Great World Writers

TWENTIETH CENTURY

EDITOR

PATRICK M. O'NEIL

Volume 1

Kōbō Abe • Chinua Achebe • Isabel Allende

W. H. Auden • Mariama Bâ • Samuel Beckett

Jorge Luis Borges • Bertolt Brecht

MARSHALL CAVENDISH

NEW YORK • TORONTO • LONDON • SYDNEY

99 White Plains Road
Tarrytown, New York 10591-9001

Website: www.marshallcavendish.com

© 2004 Marshall Cavendish Corporation

Project Editor:	Marian Armstrong
Development Editor:	Thomas McCarthy
Editorial Director:	Paul Bernabeo
Production Manager:	Michael Esposito

Designer: Patrice Sheridan

Photo Research: Anne Burns Images
Carousel Research, Inc.
Laurie Platt Winfrey
Elizabeth Meryman
Van Bucher
Cristian Peña

Indexing: AEIOU
Cynthia Crippen

Library of Congress Cataloging-in-Publication Data

Great world writers : twentieth century / editor, Patrick M. O'Neil.
p. cm.
Vol. 13 is an index volume.
Includes bibliographical references and index.
ISBN 0-7614-7469-2 (v. 1)—ISBN 0-7614-7470-6 (v. 2)—
ISBN 0-7614-7471-4 (v. 3)—ISBN 0-7614-7472-2 (v. 4)—
ISBN 0-7614-7473-0 (v. 5)—ISBN 0-7614-7474-9
(v. 6)—ISBN 0-7614-7475-7 (v. 7)—ISBN 0-7614-7476-5
(v. 8)—ISBN 0-7614-7477-3 (v. 9)—ISBN 0-7614-7478-1
(v. 10)—ISBN 0-7614-7479-X (v. 11)—ISBN 0-7614-7480-3
(v. 12)—ISBN 0-7614-7481-1 (v. 13 —ISBN 0-7614-7468-4 (set)
    1. Literature—20th century—Bio-bibliography—Dictionaries.
    2. Authors—20th century—Biography—Dictionaries.
    3. Literature—20th century—History and criticism. I.
O'Neil, Patrick M.

PN771.G73 2004
809'.04—dc21
[B]   2003040922

Printed in China

09 08 07 06 05 04   6 5 4 3 2 1

Volume 1 Illustration Credits
(a = above, b = below, l = left, r = right)

Introduction

MARILYN GADDIS ROSE

Distinguished Service Professor,
Department of Comparative Literature, Binghamton University

The 13 volumes of *Great World Writers: Twentieth Century* offer students and other interested readers an introduction to a wide variety of significant authors, both living and deceased, whose writings exemplify the extraordinary riches of literary cultures flourishing outside the United States in the last century. This set, a companion publication to *Great American Writers: Twentieth Century*, which was published in 2002, takes as its starting point the fact that the curricula of North American schools encourage students to sample the work of distinguished writers from all over the globe. *Great World Writers* exists to enable school and community libraries to offer their patrons a comprehensive resource that will expand that sample into a feast.

Writing and Reading in the Twentieth Century: An Adventure in Meaning

No reference of this size could possibly give adequate coverage to *all* twentieth-century candidates worthy of the title "great writer," and so a selection has been made, one that balances the legitimate claims of geography, culture, genre, and language. Some of the writers included herein are men and women from the first half of the century whose names are already held in high esteem. Other writers have been instrumental in shaping the literature of the past five decades. Still others are even now in their most productive years, and their work has enriched the recently closed landscape of the twentieth century while it opens the new paths that the literature of the twenty-first will tread.

Changing Meanings. The many figures in world literature of the past century, 93 of whom will be examined in these volumes, have engaged an incalculable number of readers, and the number keeps expanding. The literature itself, however, the shared property of authors and readers alike, has a significance that both endures and changes. Meaning modulates as texts cross lands and seas and survive the passage of time.

Though change in meaning is inevitable as the twenty-first century distances itself from the twentieth, it seems safe to say that those included authors who are still writing or have written recently—roughly a third—communicate precisely what they meant to say. Thus, the men and women born in the late 1930s (as, for example, Mario Vargas Llosa and Seamus Heaney were) or the 1940s (Isabel Allende and Jamaica Kincaid are two such), though the product of their own heritage, belong to the second half of the century. They speak *in* the present *to* the present. One-third (such as Thomas Mann and W. B. Yeats), however, lived their formative years in the nineteenth century, and another third (including Jean-Paul Sartre and Samuel Beckett) reached maturity prior to World War II. Rather than react to these earlier writers as their first readers did, readers of the present pick up whatever is meaningful to *them*.

The Impact of English. These writers were chosen because they are indeed read, whether they spoke in their own language or in an English voice lent them by a translator. Roughly half either wrote English natively or chose it for their medium. The other half are substantially indebted to the skill of their translators, since by the second half of the twentieth century, English had become the world's most widely used language. Some of these latter authors have had several translators, retranslation being necessary to keep their voice timely. Language, especially one as widely employed as English, is dynamic.

Still, the global pervasiveness of English is countered by its own regionalisms. Consider, for example, the Irish English of James Joyce and W. B. Yeats, the Australian English of Archie Weller and Patrick White, the Indian English of Salman Rushdie and R. K. Narayan, the Caribbean English of V. S. Naipaul and Derek Walcott, or the Nigerian English of Chinua Achebe and Wole Soyinka. In contrast, the English used by such second-language learners as Joseph Conrad, originally a Polish speaker, and Isak Dinesen, a Danish speaker, seems neutral and universal.

Criteria for Inclusion. As the foregoing makes evident, the selection of writers has been weighted in favor of those whose works are readily available and widely read in English. Most of them wrote during the period from 1920 to 1970, close enough in time for readers to recognize their urgency, far enough in time to give promise of survival, since they have already appealed to at least three generations. Most writers selected have embraced one or more "isms" (modernism, surrealism, expressionism, absurdism), but as a rule the features of these various styles have served mainly to enhance each writer's vision or voice. Every literary genre is represented, although prose fiction, the form most accessible to the solitary reader, dominates. It is assumed that the writers selected are best understood when they are interpreted in light of their biographical, historical, and geographical origin and from the perspective of their entire body of work. This is the rationale of this encyclopedia.

Writers and writing are not immune from the effects of social movements and historical currents. Literature always responds to history, if only by ignoring it, yet major cataclysms are seldom transformed into literature while they are in progress. Those experiencing battle or enduring oppression need their energies for the dangers and hardships at hand. Afterward, if they survive to testify, they may find such situations too traumatic to confront until the passage of time has had its effect.

The writers here include martyrs like Federico García Lorca and Ghassan Kanafani, combatants like André Malraux and Erich Maria Remarque, political prisoners like Václav Havel and Aleksandr Solzhenitsyn, and émigré spectators like Bertolt Brecht and Vladimir Nabokov. Indeed, in the midst of warfare and revolutions, followed or paralleled by political oppression, flight was frequently a writer's wisest choice. From the Russian Revolution in 1917 to the demolition of the Berlin Wall in 1989, flight was generally to the West, most often the United States or Europe. If the émigré writers had not chosen flight, twentieth-century literature would have been much the poorer. On the other hand, it is impossible to calculate how many other writers refused to surrender to a hopeless situation.

Some developed elaborate codes to get past censors or relied on being translated. Some even became translators in order to express themselves through the works of others.

Writers and Their Situations. Writers, on the whole, tend to speak just for themselves, less often for the collectivity; yet they have usually assumed that their own experience would be applicable to their readers or at least worthy of consideration. Take the case of two writers of the first generation represented in this set, Rabindranath Tagore and W. B. Yeats. Residents of the far-flung British colonies, they voiced the aspirations of their respective national groups as they forged their own personae. Their aspirations were positive, even noble, but by the time of the Great War and its aftermath, nationalism and self-determination had shown their destructive side. (Hermann Hesse and James Joyce, in fact, had fled to Switzerland to avoid that terrible conflict.)

Afterward, although the 1920s were euphoric for the United States and its expatriate writers were descending upon western Europe, the rest of the world was not likewise settling down to a modestly improved version of its prewar status. What in the United States is known as the Great Depression began in central Europe, where some writers and readers grew receptive to the discourse of violent action. Causes that seemed alluring at the time—Communism, Fascism, Nazism—have, with the benefit of hindsight, come to seem like delusions bent on unleashing hatred and prejudice. Their focus on long-term ends justified brutality and oppression. Only one writer included here, Luigi Pirandello of Italy, had an ambiguous relationship with his totalitarian government. Yet he was well established before the Fascists took hold, and his dramas and short stories deal with subtle interpersonal adjustments to violations of common decency.

Generally, Western writers reaching maturity in the period between the wars favored concerted action to combat perceived injustice. Sometimes, to judge from the deeds of the writers represented here, it would seem that action was not only a means but also an antidote. Albert Camus, son of French colonizers in Algeria, labored to obstruct the Nazi occupation of France during World War II. André Malraux expended himself for the left-leaning Republicans during Spain's civil war (1936–1939), yet after serving in the French resistance movement, he became a member of two cabinets of France's postwar president Charles de Gaulle, the hero of the Right.

The end of World War II saw the first application of atomic science, which changed the entire world's perspective on life and death and, as a consequence, changed the way that older books were read and new books were written. The full horror of the Holocaust was recovered. Western colonies, restive during World War II, first asserted, then implemented, their independence, with effects ranging from inconvenience to bloodbaths. Sometimes colonialism deteriorated into neocolonialism, a mere change in the axis of power. The world map, which had once been predominantly pink—or whatever color mapmakers favored for the British Empire—gave way to the tints of the cold war, with highly significant boundaries between the West (the United States and its allies) and the East (Russia and its satellites). Those boundaries crumbled tumultuously but without reconciling numerous attendant contradictions. The image of Boris Yeltsin, on August 19, 1991, standing on a tank intended for a coup, became a potent icon of effective people power. The image of a single man in shirtsleeves standing up to a tank in Tiananmen Square in Beijing, China, on June 4, 1989, however, became an icon of people power crushed. (China, still a largely censored society, has two representatives in these volumes: Chou Shu-jen, canonized by Mao Zedong, and Gao Xingjian, exiled in France.)

A Variety of Approaches. Some writers attacked problems more or less directly. In South Africa Alan Paton offered the hope of reconciliation in such books as *Cry, the Beloved Country* and *Too Late the Phalarope.* Patrick White, in *Voss,* or Gabriel García Márquez, in *One Hundred Years of Solitude,* forced readers to look at the historical perspective. Aleksandr Solzhenitsyn, in *One Day in the Life of Ivan Denisovitch,* exposed the gulag; exiled in the United States from 1971 to 1991, he returned to Russia shortly after Yeltsin's triumph. Jean-Paul Sartre explored French history through the early years of World War II from the perspective of an activist philosophy, existentialism.

For other writers, oblique references to the facts of living and dying found receptive readers. Such works, which rely on metaphor, parable, and fantasy, have been termed either engaged or escapist. This tendency to indirectness or obscurity was developed by Franz Kafka, who died in 1924 but was not really discovered and studied until after World War II, when translation into English and French brought him enthusiastic, if bewildered, readers. Writers who in the twenties and thirties had embraced surrealism and expressionism were also rediscovered, as was Aldous Huxley's *Brave New World,* a frightening account of a technologically designed society. Another Spanish civil war veteran, George Orwell, continued the tradition of allegorized totalitarianism in *Animal Farm* and predicted an eerie dystopia in *1984.* William Golding, a World War II veteran, gave a terrifying picture of human nature masquerading as a boys' story in *Lord of the Flies.* Many members of the generations reaching their full powers in the 1960s and 1970s often abandoned realist rhetoric and developed or found examples in absurdist theater or the so-called new novel. In these works bleakness and black humor, not events or characterizations, were the ties with reality. For those looking for solutions in literature, Samuel Beckett, another who had fought in the French resistance, warned in *Watt,* "no symbols where none intended." In other words, look elsewhere for help.

In the last 30 years of the century, there was a cultural realignment, a shift westward from Europe to the United States. From 1917 to 1991, mainstream literary creation in Russia and the Soviet bloc was short-circuited by a regime whose stultifying censorship paradoxically sired new forms of unauthorized and "dangerous" artistic expression and a new term to characterize the phenomenon: samizdat. Thanks in no small part to the near-complete absence of censorship in the United States, it became the new cultural center of gravity, and affirmation of this realignment quickly became the stance of the West generally as the academy and the intelligentsia realized that with political and military dominance came cultural hegemony.

Fragmentation of the monolith was inevitable, however. Beckett was Irish, and Ionesco, Romanian, not to mention that Mariama Bâ was Senegalese and Gabrielle Roy, Canadian. The energy was shifting outward. Only in literary analysis and philosophy was Europe's impact felt, the terms *deconstruction* and *postmodernism* being emblematic of its influence.

As literature became simultaneously global and regional, it could be simultaneously anti-American and responsive to American readers. The general dominance of the English language and American political hegemony are only partly responsible. English may not be easy to learn, but it is an "open" language. English speakers typically, albeit informally, both encourage the use of English and welcome nonnative speakers. This tendency has permitted globalization and regionalism to coexist productively.

Looking Ahead. Certain trends are not losing strength. In the West and in non-Western societies that have a somewhat Western educational system, more opportunities to express themselves will mean more publications by women, citizens of former colonies, and racial and sexual minorities. In teaching reading habits, there will be more effort to look for hidden agendas, covert ideologies, and inadvertent bias.

This situation will be healthy for literature, veritably guaranteeing that the writers in *Great World Writers: Twentieth Century* will continue to find an audience. Altered reading habits will only serve to reveal the incredible clairvoyance of masterworks that embody meanings their authors, however inadvertently, "encoded," over and above their own announced intentions or their readers' obsessions.

A Reader's Guide to the Organization of This Encyclopedia

Great World Writers: Twentieth Century reflects the breadth of world literature in both its diversity and its unifying elements. Each article examines the life and works of an individual author in a treatment that combines fresh scholarly assessment with a wealth of visual material ranging from an author's own snapshots to reproductions of great works of art. While this set presents much unfamiliar information, it does so in a regular pattern that allows its readers to examine each author's life and professional career in segments that are separate from those in which close consideration is given to major and less important works. This framework also makes room for display materials that put an abundance of factual information in an accessible format.

Each article begins with a one-page summary that identifies the author and outlines his or her significance. Next comes an extended examination of the most important events in the author's life; this section includes a detailed chronology and, wherever appropriate, a display listing films adapted from the author's books, stories, or plays. "The Writer's Life" is followed by another long section, "The Writer's Work," which deals with recurrent themes and issues, modes of character development, and other relevant matters. This section typically embodies a look at the inspirations that shaped the writer's work—people, places, books, movements, events, or whatever else may be germane. The section includes a detailed list of the writer's published works and concludes with a critical bibliography.

The next section, "Reader's Guide to Major Works," focuses as a rule on two to four of the writer's most notable and representative published works. In each case themes, issues, and plot are examined to the extent appropriate, and pertinent analysis follows. Sources for further study conclude the discussion of each title. "Other Works," the section that follows, summarizes in less detail one or more of the author's other significant publications.

A list of resources concludes each article. This section is designed to allow readers to supplement their knowledge of the writer by providing information on manuscript collections, archives, societies, memorials, publications, and miscellaneous but important bibliographical data. Related Web addresses are included wherever they are available, and the use of the Internet as a research tool is encouraged and assisted.

A special merit of these volumes lies in a group of supplementary essays that cover, outside of the normal article structure, areas or issues of potentially great interest to contemporary students and other readers. About a third of the articles—those on writers whose life and work offer especially rich scope for supplementation—include an essay of this sort.

Each of the first 12 volumes closes with a two-page index to the titles of the works of literature and visual art found in that volume. Indexing art along with literature serves to underline the inseparability of the graphic and verbal aspects of this encyclopedia. It also facilitates research for readers who have a special or even a primary interest in the visual arts.

Volume 13, the Index volume, contains a wealth of supporting information, both complementary and supplementary to what has gone before. A glossary defines the many terms associated with events and movements that formed the writers' outlook and informed their work. Analytical lists and indexes abound. The former category includes a list of the winners of the Nobel Prize for literature and a list of writers grouped by the genres they wrote in; there is also a list of resources for further study. In the latter category, writers, literary works and characters, related films, visual arts and artists, and even people, places, movements, and events mentioned in the first 12 volumes are all separately indexed. The contributors, the editors, and the publisher of *Great World Writers: Twentieth Century* consider this a rich and important work, and the manifold resources of the Index volume aim at assisting readers to make full use of its treasures.

Contributors

Hena Ahmad
Truman State University

Jessica Allen
University of Washington

Kristine J. Anderson
Purdue University

Katherine Bacon
Broome Community College, SUNY

Philip Bader
Pasadena, CA

Aida A. Bamia
University of Florida

Thomas F. Bertonneau
State University of New York at Oswego

Brian Black
Pennsylvania State University

Zack Bowen
University of Miami

Anthony Bukoski
University of Wisconsin–Superior

Todd Burrell
New York University

Irene J. Byrnes
Broome Community College, SUNY

Charles A. Carpenter
Binghamton University

David Castronuovo
Middlebury College

Joe R. Christopher
Tarleton State University

Gloria Bodtorf Clark
Pennsylvania State University

June E. Deery
Rensselaer Polytechnic Institute

Mary E. Donnelly
Broome Community College, SUNY

Martha Lamkin Fenty
Broome Community College, SUNY

Daniel Horace Fernald
Georgia College and State University

Thomas Fleming
The Rockford Institute

Deborah A. Folaron
New York, NY

Kris Fresonke
Adelphi University

Marketa Goetz-Stankiewicz
University of British Columbia

Andrew J. Haggerty
Broome Community College, SUNY

Martin Holman
Berea College

Michael Huff
Binghamton University

K. L. A. Hyatt
Pasadena, CA

Howard A. Kerner
Polk Community College

Harold Koster
Broome Community College, SUNY

Tom M. Lansford
University of Southern Mississippi

Heather Levy
Binghamton University

Steven Luckert
Burtonsville, MD

Richard Major
New York, NY

Patrick A. McCarthy
University of Miami

Heather McCloud-Huff
Binghamton University

Michelle E. Moore
College of DuPage

Joseph A. Murphy
University of Florida

John G. Peters
University of North Texas

Karen M. Radell
Central Michigan University

Dana Renga
Colorado College

Carlos Rojas
University of Florida

Marilyn Gaddis Rose
Binghamton University

Frank A. Salamone
Iona College

Virginia Salamone
White Plains, NY

Maureen Salzer
University of Wisconsin–Superior

Renée T. Schatteman
Georgia State University

Thomas Schnellbächer
Berlin Free University

Ben Shefftz
South Lake Tahoe, CA

Melvin Shefftz
Binghamton University

William H. Snyder
Binghamton University

Lorena Terando
New York University

Robert J. Toole
Barry University

Michael VanDussen
Batavia, NY

W. Warren Wagar
Binghamton University

Douglas J. Weatherford
Brigham Young University

Charles E. Williams
Arlington, VA

Amy Zalman
New York University

Contents

Kōbō Abe

BORN: March 7, 1924, Tokyo, Japan
DIED: January 22, 1993, Tokyo, Japan
IDENTIFICATION: One of the first post–World War II Japanese writers to win international acclaim, writing novels and plays that employ a many-layered fantastic realism.

SIGNIFICANCE: Kōbō Abe helped reshape postwar Japanese literature, particularly following the success of his 1962 novel *Suna no onna* (*The Woman in the Dunes*). His characteristic style, which comes over well in translation, conveys dizzying narrative spaces through a straightforward syntax. Though Abe was a communist at the beginning of his career, he enjoyed overseas popularity on both sides of the Iron Curtain. Toward the end of his life, he was rumored to be a leading candidate for the Nobel Prize in literature. Since his death his best-known works, both in Japan and abroad, remain the novels he wrote in the 1960s.

Kimifusa Abe (Kōbō, the more commonly used form of his name, is an alternative reading of the same Japanese characters) was born in Tokyo but spent the first 16 years of his life mainly in Mukden, Manchuria. This semicolonial town featured a Japanese medical school, where his father was an assistant professor. His mother had studied Japanese literature and been involved in the Japanese proletarian literature movement of the 1920s. Abe himself was more interested in science than in literature as a boy.

The War Years. From 1940 Abe attended a Tokyo high school. His reading at this stage incorporated more philosophy than literature and favored Western rather than Japanese authors. He retained these reading habits after war broke out in 1941 and after he became a medical student at the elite Tokyo University in 1942.

At the end of 1944, hearing that Japan's defeat was imminent, Abe and a friend decided to make their way to Manchuria, preferring to be with their families in Mukden rather than in

Tokyo when the war ended. Faking a medical certificate with a diagnosis of tuberculosis, Abe was granted formal leave from the university. Ironically, his friend later died from this disease after fleeing in turn from Mukden. (The protagonist of Abe's first novel is a Japanese lost on the Asian continent and suffering from tuberculosis.) Abe's father died in Manchuria while treating the victims of a typhoid epidemic. The rest of the family was repatriated at the end of 1946.

Literary Debut. Returning to Tokyo in 1947 to finish his university studies, Abe actually spent more time writing literature than studying. He was quickly drawn into the lively postwar arts scene, where he met and married the painter Machiko Yamada (known professionally as Machi Abe), who worked closely with him throughout his career. In 1947 he published a mimeographed book of poems and wrote his debut novel, *Owarishi michi no shirube ni* (To Mark the End of the Road). He then showed the novel manuscript to his former high school German teacher, who was mentor to some leading writers of the "postwar faction," the most vociferous literary reformers of that time. The resulting serialization of the novel was discontinued after one installment, but it was published as Abe's first commercial book in 1948. He graduated the same year but never practiced as a doctor.

Looking back over the first postwar decade, Abe remembered passing rapidly through three phases: existentialist, surrealist, and then communist. He was also involved with a succession of increasingly politicized artists' groups. Probably during 1951 he joined the radical "mainstream faction" of the Japan Communist

Telephone poles and rickshaws can be found in this street scene from the Walled Town section of Mukden (now Shenyang) in the early twentieth century. Abe grew up in the city, the largest in Manchuria, during Japan's brief time as Manchuria's overlord. Early life as an exile of sorts may have inspired his fascination with lost people and empty landscapes. "I am a man without a home," he once said.

Party (JCP). Whether or not Abe fully espoused the party line that Japan was a U.S. colony, he was certainly a dedicated party campaigner. The debates within left-wing movements sharpened both his political and his literary awareness. It is no coincidence that the same year also saw him receiving the prestigious Akutagawa Prize for his first story collection, *Kabe (Walls)*.

In 1955, a year that was characterized by consolidation across the Japanese political spectrum, Abe was elected to the executive committee of the New Japan Literature Association, the main nationwide organization for left-wing writers. In 1956 he represented New Japan at the Czechoslovakian Writers Congress, going on to spend three months traveling mainly in eastern Europe. In his travel account *Tōō o yuku* (Through Eastern Europe), published in 1957, he openly criticized the JCP for refusing to acknowledge that there must be social contradictions even in socialist societies. In 1962 he was one of 28 communist writers expelled from the party in response to their public criticism of the party.

As a Major Author. It was immediately after this expulsion that Abe wrote the novel that was to establish him as a mature writer both at home and overseas, *The Woman in the Dunes*. At the same time he suspended virtually all activity in large-scale national organizations.

In the 1950s Abe had begun writing dramas for stage and radio as well as screenplays. He also became increasingly involved in acting theory and taught an acting course at a Tokyo college. It was mainly with students from this course that he formed his own theater troupe, the Kōbō Abe Studio, in 1973. In fact, Abe, who also had collections of his photographs published, was as interested in the visual aspect of drama as in dialogue. The later productions of the studio, before the group disbanded in 1979, were closer to dance theater than to conventional drama.

From the 1980s Abe's output decreased markedly, perhaps because of an abrupt decline in his health. His last two novels were received respectfully but without enthusiasm.

FILMS BASED ON ABE'S WORKS

1964 *Woman in the Dunes*

1966 *The Face of Another*

1968 *The Ruined Map*

1988 *Friends*

Abe in the prime of life. One of Japan's best-known writers since World War II, he wrote about individuals trapped by the absurd, but he was anything but passive when it came to his work. Branching out from literature to drama, he eventually founded a troupe that relentlessly drilled already accomplished actors as Abe explored his idea of a theater that moved beyond words to pure sensation.

Politics and the Human Condition. Kōbō Abe began writing at a time of personal (and collective) crisis, and it is descriptions of existential despair and alienation (for example, in his first novel, coming to terms with the death of his friend) that characterize his early works. The avant-garde fables that he began writing soon afterward show a playful delight in chaos while also continuing to treat existential despair. His early stories abound in striking images, such as the narrator-protagonist coming undone like a piece of knitting in "Akai mayu" ("Red Cocoon," 1951). For Abe, such "deformations" arouse pleasure because they give expression to collective neuroses caused by social pressure to conform.

Abe was always a disciplined revolutionary. He incorporated into his program the norms of socialist realism and documentarism demanded by communist discourse, despite his contempt for naive realism. He was a critical realist whose works challenge the audience not to believe its eyes. The questioning of everyday reality is also what interested Abe in science fiction, which he started writing in the mid-1950s.

Genres. Having published *Dai-yon kampyoki* (*Inter Ice Age Four*) (1959), the first Japanese science fiction novel, Abe wrote nothing else strictly in this genre, always wary of the complacency of existing genres. However, he certainly strove to write popular and accessible prose, and his work has a unique sensual quality. In his mature novels striking images are often conveyed by inner monologue ("[. . .] my heart was transformed into a red, heart-shaped ice bag"; *Moetsukita chizu [The Ruined Map]*). In the theater Abe liked to use song and dance acts, and he frequently demanded acrobatic feats of his actors.

Metaphor and Social Commitment. Abe's best work is characterized by highly suggestive metaphors that resist reduction to a

Abe (left) accepts an honorary doctorate from Columbia University in New York City in 1975. American scholar and translator Donald Keene, not in the photograph, the namesake for Columbia University's Donald Keene Center for Japanese Culture, has called Abe a writer of "world stature."

HIGHLIGHTS IN ABE'S LIFE

1924 Kōbō Abe is born in Tokyo.

1925 Moves with family to Mukden, Manchuria.

1940 Attends high school in Tokyo.

1942 Enrolls as medical student at Tokyo University.

1944 With a friend leaves Tokyo for Mukden.

1946 Is repatriated.

1947 Begins writing for publication; marries Machiko Yamada.

1948 First novel, *Owarishi michi no shirube ni,* is published; Abe graduates from Tokyo University.

1951 Joins Japan Communist Party (JCP); receives Akutagawa Prize.

1956 Travels for three months in eastern Europe and France; travel account leads to conflict with JCP.

1962 Abe is expelled from JCP; *The Woman in the Dunes* wins national acclaim.

1964 *The Woman in the Dunes* is published in the United States; film version wins prize at Cannes Film Festival.

1973 Abe launches theater troupe, Kōbō Abe Studio.

1975 Receives honorary doctorate from Columbia University.

1979 Abe Studio disbands.

1990 Abe is hospitalized for two months.

1991 Last novel, *Kangaru noto (Kangaroo Notebook),* is published.

1993 Abe dies from heart failure.

particular meaning, such as the sand in *The Woman in the Dunes*. Not only did this use of metaphor enable Abe to reach beyond Japan, it was in fact developed to appeal to popular expectations of reality—that is, the illusion of reality—only to show how unreliable these expectations are.

BIBLIOGRAPHY

Bolton, Christopher. "Science and Fiction in the Work of Abe Kōbō." Ph.D. diss., Stanford University, 1999.

Currie, William J. "Metaphors of Alienation. The Fiction of Abe, Beckett and Kafka." Ph.D. diss., University of Michigan, 1973.

Dworkin, Andrea. "Skinless." In *Intercourse*. New York: Free Press, 1987.

Shields, Nancy K. *Fake Fish. The Theater of Kobo Abe*. New York and Tokyo: Weatherhill, 1996.

Yamanouchi, Hisaaki. "The Search for Identity in Contemporary Japanese Literature." In *Modern Japan: Aspects of History, Literature and Society,* edited by W. G. Beasley. London: Allen and Unwin, 1975.

Reader's Guide to Major Works

THE WOMAN IN THE DUNES

Genre: Novel
Subgenres: Fantastic adventure; fictional documentary
Published: Tokyo, 1962
Time period: 1955–1962
Setting: A landlocked former fishing village

Themes and Issues. The sand of the title (a literal translation would be "The Sand Woman") stands for many things: for a material world that passes over humanity in crushing waves; for a female landscape to be cultivated; for the masses resisting political instrumentalization, and so on. The narrative both reflects contemporary social changes and acts out the archetypal drama of mankind and nature.

The Plot. A man has been declared dead seven years after being reported missing. He is a schoolteacher and insect collector who made a day trip from Tokyo to a certain sand dune landscape hoping to find an unknown mutation of a particular beetle. Told that he has missed the last bus, he is led to a house between the dunes, reached via a rope ladder. In the morning the ladder is gone. He finds out he has been trapped to replace the husband of a young widow; his task is to help her clear the sand every day in order to preserve the house—and to have children with her. After numerous unsuccessful escape attempts, he provisionally settles into his new life. Left alone as the woman is taken to a hospital with pregnancy complications, he decides consciously to postpone escape.

Analysis. The protagonist, an average urban male intellectual, is fascinated in an abstract way by the dune wilderness and the fluid properties of sand. The landscape is actually a miniature desert and is depriving a former fishing village of its traditional livelihood and turning it into a desperate, marginal, parasitic community. The novel's conclusion is not the product of resignation, for the protagonist realizes that his neurotic quest for liberty would only lead him back to the constraints of the urban society he was originally trying to escape. This ending has implications not only within the novel but for society as well, since, through literature, the

The protagonist of *Woman in the Dunes,* played by Eiji Okada, marches forward into a trap. He already seems to have entered limbo thanks to the "ceaseless movement" of the sand: "As long as the winds blew, the rivers flowed, and the seas stirred, sand would be borne grain by grain from the earth, and like a living being it would creep everywhere. The sands never rested," wrote Abe in his novel. Director Hiroshi Teshigahara's film version of the work cost $100,000 and won the Grand Jury Prize at Cannes in 1964.

protagonist's realization could influence a wide audience.

SOURCES FOR FURTHER STUDY

Dissanayake, Wimal. "Self, Place and Body in *The Woman in the Dunes.*" In *Literary Relations East and West,* vol. 3, edited by J. Toyama and N. Ochner. Honolulu: University of Hawaii at Manoa Press, 1990.

Kimball, Arthur G. "Identity Found: *Suna no onna.*" In *Crisis in Identity and the Contemporary Japanese Novel.* Rutland, VT: Tuttle, 1962.

Treat, John Whittier. "The Woman in the Dunes." In *Masterworks of Asian Literature in Comparative Perspective. A Guide for Teaching,* edited by B. Stoler Miller. Armonk, NY: Sharpe, 1994.

THE FACE OF ANOTHER

Genre: Novel
Subgenres: Domestic drama; horror

Published: Tokyo, 1964
Time period: Contemporary (year unspecified)
Setting: Tokyo

Themes and Issues. Abe's great theme was the alienating yet creative effect of urban civilization on human beings. In *The Face of Another (Tanin no kao),* the narrator-protagonist is a monster, whose latent paranoia is worsened by his desperation to maintain normality. For Abe, such paranoia was a medium to reveal hidden social conflicts, seen as the motors of change.

The Plot. In a laboratory accident the protagonist's facial skin has been disfigured. His wife (to whom the narrative is addressed in diary form) has since turned away from his advances. Assuming that

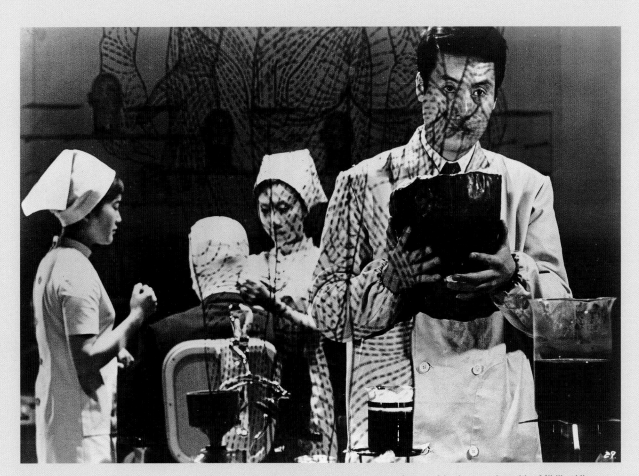

The bandaged Mr. Okuyama, portrayed by actor Tatsuya Nakadai, awaits a new face as his doctor, played by Mikijiro Hira, weighs the situation. In 1966 *The Face of Another* followed *The Woman in the Dunes* to become the second of Abe's novels to be filmed by director Hiroshi Teshigahara. Two years later he directed the film version of Abe's novel *The Ruined Map*. Abe wrote the screenplays for all three.

In his childhood Abe knew the semidesert landscapes and the frontier-town atmosphere of semicolonial Manchuria, both of which were very different from Japanese environments. Echoes of both can be sensed throughout his work. His interest in the sciences echoes that of his father, for whom he has expressed admiration. About his mother and her involvement in the proletarian literature movement he has written little.

Most of Abe's explicit literary models were Western. Kafka is most often cited, but earlier literary enthusiasm was inspired by Edgar Allan Poe, Fyodor Dostoyevsky, and Rainer Maria Rilke. In philosophical terms Abe repeatedly declined to be classified, but it can be said that the existential themes of his early work are soon joined, though certainly not replaced, by socialism and Marxist materialism.

this rejection is due to his lack of a face, he makes a mask and then seduces her as a stranger. The masked seduction is an apparent success, but the narrator finally becomes insanely jealous of his own creation. At the same time his wife leaves him: replying in his notebooks, she reveals that she had soon recognized him through his behavior and accuses him of using the mask to escape from himself, not to communicate.

Analysis. Besides being about the function of the face in social communication, *The Face of Another* is an allegory of authorship. For Abe, creativity was a struggle between the irrational living impulses (represented by the narrator) and the dead but communicative surface (mask or text). The novel ends in a schizophrenic rupture of the two.

FRIENDS
Genre: Play
Subgenre: Didactic black comedy with musical elements
Published: Tokyo, 1967
Time period: Not specified
Setting: Mostly inside an urban bachelor's apartment

Themes and Issues. *Friends (Tomoclachi)* plays through the ideology of the family.

Reversing the *Woman in the Dunes* scenario, the single male is confronted with the parasitic "family" on his own territory.

In Abe's 1967 play *Friends* a man's life is invaded until he's reduced to a prisoner in a cage. "But running away means disappearing," he's told. "And that's a much more frightening thing than you suppose. You don't think we could expose you to such a danger, knowing how frightening it is to disappear." Artist Terry Long takes imprisonment to its ultimate point with *Figure Inside Box, Number 2*.

LONG FICTION

1948 Owarishi michi no shirube ni
1959 Inter Ice Age Four
1962 The Woman in the Dunes
1964 The Face of Another
1967 The Ruined Map
1973 The Box Man
1977 Mikkai (Secret Rendezvous)
1984 Hakobune sakuramaru (The Ark Sakura)
1991 Kangaroo Notebook

SHORT FICTION COLLECTIONS

1951 Walls
1956 R 62 no hatsumei (The invention of R 62)

1964 Mukankei na shi (An irrelevant death)

NONFICTION

1957 Tōō o yuku (Through Eastern Europe) (travel account)
1957 Mōjū no kokoro ni keisanki no te o (With the Heart of a Wild Beast and a Hand like a Calculating Machine) (essays)
1965 Sabaku no shisō (The Philosophy of the Desert) (essays)

PLAYS

1955 Seifuku (The uniform)
1956 Mimi (The ear) (radio)

1957 Kuchi (The mouth) (radio)
1958 The Ghost Is Here
1959 Shijin no shōgai (The life of a poet) (TV)
1965 Mokugekisha (The eyewitness) (TV)
1967 Friends
1969 Bo ni natta otoko (The man who turned into a stick)
1971–1978 Gaido bukku (guide-book), parts 1–4
1977–1979 Imēji no tenrankai (An exhibition of pictures), parts 1–3

SCREENPLAYS

1964 Woman in the Dunes
1966 The Face of Another
1968 The Ruined Map

The Plot. An eight-member family suddenly visits the apartment of the protagonist. Because there is no damage and the landlady will not testify that the intruders are there against her will, all attempts to evict them fail. The man's fiancée, herself a single working woman, is seduced by one of the sons. Matters come to a head when the man himself starts to become friendly with the eldest daughter and the other adult daughter accuses them of planning to elope. To "cure" him of his desire for freedom, he is imprisoned in a cage. However, the second daughter, pitying him because she sees no hope for a cure, poisons him.

Analysis. Abe's premise is that in urban society, the family exists only as an abstract idea. However, the ideology of the family is all the stronger for the absence of the real thing. Abe sees ideologies (which he compares to ghosts) as emerging inevitably from one of the most basic human impulses: The desire to name things. Ideologies do not represent reality, but they change it.

Other Works

"THE CRIME OF S. KARMA" (1951). In "The Crime of S. Karma," the prizewinning short story in *Walls*, the protagonist's genuine name has been stolen by his business card, and he embarks on a surreal odyssey to get it back. At the end he is transformed into a wall (the embodiment of civilization), stretching across a barren landscape.

THE GHOST IS HERE (1958/1970). In this musical play (original title, *Yûrei wa koka ni iru*), an invisible and inaudible ghost is the principal character. Two men, one accompanied by a dead comrade in arms, buy unwanted photographs of the dead. Then, arousing fears by suggesting that the dead are upset by the loss of their faces, they sell back the photographs at a profit. The town prospers as a result of the "ghost economy."

INTER ICE AGE FOUR (1959). Responding to reports about a Soviet computer designed to make predictions, a rival program is started in Japan. However, the government then forbids political predictions. The machine responds by envisioning the submersion of most landmasses. Moreover, it initiates a secret program to develop water-breathing mammals, including humans. The narrator, who heads the computer project, is not informed of this plan, since the machine predicts his opposition to it. He is condemned to death by a tribunal, but before his execution, he is shown a computer-generated vision of a submarine civilization.

THE BOX MAN (1973). *The Box Man (Hako otoko)* is also the narrator's term for himself. He wears a cardboard box that covers his head, face, arms, and genitals and thus effectively prevents his having any direct interaction with other humans. From the outside he is faceless and indistinguishable from other box men.

In Abe's short story "The Crime of S. Karma" the hero doesn't like his chances when he ponders getting back his identity from a mutinous business card: "If it came to blows, I could easily handle a piece of paper, however fine the quality, but my lack of a name was a serious disadvantage. The law might very well take the card's side. Especially considering that my name had not been stolen, but had gotten up and left of its own volition." The figure in Alan Magee's *Schistos,* created in 1988, seems to be in a similarly torn state of mind.

Abe keeps the reader guessing who the narrator is and what in the narrative is memory, hallucination, a lie, or playful fiction. There is a plausible solution, but it is hidden.

Resources

Though there is limited information on Abe on the Internet, much of it is worthwhile.

Abe Kobo Web Site. Assembled by Mark Gibeau, this site contains an annotated bibliography, a biographical table, links, and detailed summaries of Abe's works, some of which are not available in English (www.ibiblio.org/abekobo/index.html).

Horagai. This on-line magazine is the biggest Japanese Abe Web site. The English version is small and not often updated, but it is still worth consulting (www.horagai.com/english.html).

The Modern Word. This large site deals with twentieth-century experimental literature. It contains an essay on Abe, with links and a list of works in translation (www.themodernword.com/scriptorium/abe.html).

THOMAS SCHNELLBÄCHER

Chinua Achebe

BORN: November 16, 1930, Ogidi, Nigeria

IDENTIFICATION: Author of novels, essays, poems, and short stories, as well as a literary and social critic, the founder and editor of two journals, a professor, and a lecturer.

SIGNIFICANCE: One of the most important African writers of his generation, Chinua Achebe has had a huge influence on the way African literature has been received in Europe and the United States. As manifest in both fiction and nonfiction, his critique of European representations of native peoples has been a touchstone for the discipline of postcolonial studies and indeed constitutes a fresh examination of the nature of the entire colonial enterprise. Achebe, raised in both the European colonial environment and the traditional Ibo society of his native Nigeria, has eloquently represented the tensions both within and between these two worlds.

Chinua Achebe (his full name is Albert Chinualumogu Achebe) was born to ethnic Ibo (or Igbo) parents on November 16, 1930, in Ogidi, Nigeria. His father, Isaiah Okafor Achebe, a catechist for the Church Missionary Society, traveled all over eastern Nigeria, with his wife, Janet Iloegbunam, and their children in tow. When Chinua, the fifth of six children, was only five, Isaiah retired, and he and the family returned to live in their ancestral town of Ogidi permanently. There the young Achebe experienced a still largely traditional culture, where old Ibo folktales and proverbs were taught to children by their mother.

Education. Achebe's early education was in the Church Missionary Society school in Ogidi. At 8 he began to learn English, and at 14 he was sent to the prestigious government secondary school in Umuahia. By his own account he was a voracious reader; in his school library, stocked with the masterworks of European literature, he became fascinated by the power of literature. In 1948, at age 18, he entered University College, Ibadan, a new college closely modeled after the University of London. At that time Achebe rejected his British name, Albert, in favor of his indigenous name, which means "my spirit come fight for

"The writer who is not in trouble with the king is in trouble with his work," said Achebe, seen here in Philadelphia in 1988, when he was the Charles P. Stevenson Jr. Professor of Languages and Literature at Bard College in Annandale-on-Hudson, New York. "In the West, it's assumed that you can be a writer and neutral. This is not possible in Nigeria." Achebe's words rang true when the Nigerian government executed the writer Ken Saro-Wiwa and eight others. Saro-Wiwa's plays, novels, and essays were often thinly veiled attacks on the Nigerian government for its hand in exploiting the nation's rich oil reserves.

me." After spending one unhappy year studying medicine, Achebe switched to literature. He became a regular contributor to the *University Herald* and decided that he wanted to write professionally. He took an honors degree in 1953.

Early Professional Life. When Achebe left college, his first employment was in broadcasting, where he worked for several years. As a broadcaster in the years preceding Nigerian independence, Achebe was more than just a technical or administrative employee. He understood that he had the power to create a sense of community and shared history among Nigeria's disparate peoples. He traveled widely throughout the country and explicitly used his posts—first as head of the talks section and then as head of the Voice of Nigeria—for nation building. At the same time he wrote prolifically and produced novels in 1958, 1960, 1964, and 1966.

Marriage and Family. In 1961 Achebe married Christie Chinwe Okoli, a psychologist, who took her degree in London. They have had four children: Chinelo, a daughter, born in 1962; Ikechukwu, a son, born in 1964; Chidi, a son, born in 1967; and Nwando, a daughter, born in 1970. As of 2002, Christie Achebe, who earned a doctorate in education, was a visiting professor of psychology at Bard College.

Biafran War. After Nigeria achieved independence in 1960, the resulting volatile political situation led to various regional conflicts, some political, some armed. Different ethnic groups dominated different regions of the country, and each struggled for control of the central government in the capital of Lagos. Severe corruption marked the 1965 election, after which

Refugees, mostly children, flee from the turmoil sparked by the Biafran War. During the conflict, which lasted from 1967 to 1970, Achebe supported the east, the predominantly Ibo, Biafran side, which would ultimately lose the war. He joined the Biafran Ministry of Information and represented Biafra as a diplomat.

military officers, many of them Ibo, seized power in January 1966 and installed Major General Johnson Aguiyi-Ironsi, an Ibo, as head of state and effectively ended the first Nigerian republic. When this group was overthrown by another military coup in July under the leadership of General Gowon, Achebe's cousin, who was a military officer, was executed by the new anti-Ibo forces. The seriousness of his situation forced Achebe into hiding with his wife and two small children before they fled Lagos altogether.

The conflict that followed began when the eastern region, calling itself Biafra, attempted to secede from Nigeria in 1967. Primarily because the southeastern section of the nation

HIGHLIGHTS IN ACHEBE'S LIFE

1930   Chinua Achebe is born in Ogidi, an Ibo community in eastern Nigeria.

1948   Enters University College, Ibadan.

1953   Earns bachelor's degree; joins Nigerian Broadcasting Service.

1956   Travels to London; trains with the British Broadcasting Corporation.

1958   Publishes *Thing Fall Apart.*

1960   Nigeria gains independence; *No Longer at Ease* is published.

1961   Achebe is named director of the BBC's Voice of Nigeria; marries Christie Chinwe Okoli.

1964   Publishes *Arrow of God.*

1966   Is forced to leave Lagos and return to eastern Nigeria; publishes *A Man of the People.*

1967   Nigerian Civil War breaks out; Achebe travels widely in support of Biafran independence.

1971   Publishes *Beware Soul Brother;* founds *Okike: An African Journal of New Writing.*

1972   Publishes *Girls at War and Other Stories;* is awarded Commonwealth Poetry Prize for *Beware Soul Brother.*

1972–1976   Lives and teaches in the United States.

1976   Returns to Nigeria to teach at the University of Nigeria in Nsukka.

1979   Is awarded the Nigerian National Merit Award and the Order of the Federal Republic.

1982   Edits *Aka Weta,* an anthology of verse, with Obiora Udechukwu.

1983   Is appointed deputy national president of the People's Redemption Party; publishes *The Trouble with Nigeria.*

1984   Founds *Uwa ndi Igbo: A Journal of Igbo Life and Culture.*

1987   Publishes *Anthills of the Savannah;* is a finalist for the prestigious Booker Prize.

1988   Publishes *Hopes and Impediments.*

1990   Is injured in an automobile accident and is paralyzed from the waist down.

2000   Publishes *Home and Exile.*

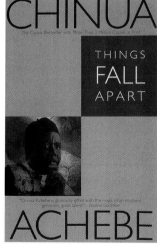

Achebe is shown in this 1999 photograph outside his home in Ogidi in eastern Nigeria. The novelist was injured in a car crash in 1990, which left him paralyzed from the waist down.

national spokesman for the Biafran cause and traveled throughout Africa, Europe, and the Western Hemisphere. His diplomatic efforts did not pay off, however: military defeat in 1970 ended all hopes of Biafran independence.

Life in America. After the defeat of Biafra, Achebe returned to his creative work, publishing several volumes of short works in the next few years. Beginning in 1972, he taught literature, moving back and forth from American to Nigerian universities. He continued to write, though his focus at this point turned to the essay, including literary criticism and political commentary. Nigeria continued to be plagued by political trauma; brief flowerings of democratic government were crushed by the military several times in the 1970s and 1980s. Achebe reflected on these developments in two related volumes: the 1983 nonfiction work *The Trouble with Nigeria* and the 1987 novel *Anthills of the Savannah.*

In 1990 Achebe was seriously injured in an automobile accident outside Lagos that left him paralyzed below the waist. He was flown to Europe for treatment and soon after accepted an endowed chair at Bard College. Though he expected a short tenure, he was still affiliated with Bard in 2002. In 1999 he returned to Nigeria for the first time in a decade, a bittersweet experience. While there he met the first civilian leader Nigeria had had in many years, Olusegun Obasanjo, and expressed some hope for the future. As of 2002 Achebe continued to be an active commentator on the African scene and to teach and lecture widely.

was rich in oil, secession was met with military attempts to forcibly reintegrate Biafra into Nigeria. From 1967 to 1970, war raged, financed largely by foreign governments interested in the oil reserves.

The Biafran War (also called the Nigerian Civil War) engendered great suffering. The wholesale slaughter of the rebellious Ibo, both in the eastern region and in other parts of Nigeria, was only part of the crisis: large-scale famine and disease also pushed up the death toll. Achebe became an inter-

The major theme of Chinua Achebe's fiction might best be described as "the colonial encounter: before, during, and after." His precolonial Nigeria is not an idealized pastoral world, but neither is it the savage wilderness represented by so many European writers. The Ibo are intelligent, thoughtful, and reasonable. They live according to a set of socially accepted tenets, and their behavior generally makes sense according to those tenets. At the same time, one can see how Achebe's disaffected characters can be attracted by the unfamiliar aspects of English society, particularly Christianity.

Effects of Colonialism.
The appeal of Christianity in the colonial encounter is particularly important to Achebe: he has called it "the psychology of religious imperialism." In *Things Fall Apart,* Okonkwo loses his son to Christianity. In *Arrow of God*, the Ibo priest Ezelulu struggles to maintain the faith of the members of his flock in the old ways and the old gods. He destroys them by demanding an unreasonable sacrifice that may lead to famine, yet he is unsure whether it is he or the god who speaks through him that is causing the crisis. In an animist society the future of the people depends on their faith: if the gods are angry, it is not the individuals who have abandoned them who will be punished, it is the whole village. At the same time Achebe has said that the

Ibo were particularly vulnerable to this so-called religious imperialism because they had never impressed their own religion upon others and did not understand why anyone would do such a thing. As a village elder says to the British missionary in *Things Fall Apart*, "it is good for a man to follow the gods of his fathers."

Perhaps the most important element of Achebe's fiction is the sense of dualism engendered by colonialism. It is not possible,

Among Achebe's principal preoccupations as a novelist are the effects of colonialism and the often disastrous results of two cultures colliding. Mark Tansey's 1994 artwork *Continental Divide* captures this duality in which the long, elegantly appointed table stands as a border or barrier in stark contrast to the growth of the forest teeming beyond.

he seems to suggest, for any colonial subject to maintain one identity, native or foreign, Ibo or English. The nature of the colonial encounter creates a sense of living in two worlds at once. It is a mark of the philosophical sophistication of the Ibo that they can negotiate this duality more easily than their colonizers can. As the Ibo proverb says, "Wherever one thing stands, another stands beside it." Achebe reserves his most biting characterizations for the British colonizers, religious and civil, whose goal it is to unify Nigeria by creating a single, British society. Nigerians who adopt a more British perspective, such as Obi Okonkwo in *No Longer at Ease*, are condemned to suffer both from the prejudices of their white rulers and from the expectations of their traditional villages.

Postcolonial Nigeria. In the postcolonial period Nigeria fares little better in Achebe's fiction (or indeed in history). Instead of restoring a lost wholeness, the leaders of postcolonial Nigeria that Achebe focuses on are petty power brokers engaged in vicious struggles for pitiful rewards and ruthless megalomaniacs who surround themselves with yes-men. In *Man of the People* the conflict between Odili and Nanga reveals how far Nigeria has come from the communal values of the village without yet having adopted the disinterested philanthropy of the British. Like *No Longer at Ease, Man of the People* is set in a world where corruption is taken for granted, but without any sense of external control, it has run rampant. In *Anthills of the Savannah* even the most able leaders cannot help turning on their closest allies in the struggle to maintain power. Any criticism is treason, and the desire for absolute power crushes both those who suffer under it and those who wield it.

The language of Achebe's major fictional works is English, but many of the words, proverbs, and stories come straight out of the Ibo oral tradition. Among the Ibo, as Achebe writes in *Things Fall Apart*, conversation is an art. In the novel talk is sprinkled with folk stories that illustrate widely accepted social wisdom; proverbs and specific verbal constructions suggest to readers that the text is not originally in English but is a translation of a language they could not understand. In that sense the form of Achebe's novels, in that they *are* written in English, attests to the success of the colonial project even as he represents the world it has replaced.

One important quality of Achebe's work is its unequivocal commitment to the artist's responsibility to the community. Achebe has long been dedicated to representing the world of his childhood and youth and has said that he has trouble writing about Nigeria when he is not there. He recognizes, too, the power of storytelling as a social act that gives meaning to a people's history. As a village elder says in *Anthills of the Savannah*, "The story is our escort; without it, we are blind." The storyteller needs the community, but the community also needs the storyteller.

BIBLIOGRAPHY

Carroll, David. *Chinua Achebe.* New York: Twayne, 1970.

Emenyonu. *The Rise of the Igbo Novel.* Ibadan, Nigeria: Oxford University Press, 1978.

Glenn, Ian. "Heroic Failure in the Novels of Achebe." *English in Africa* 12, no. 1 (1985): 11–27.

Innes, C. L. *Chinua Achebe.* Cambridge Studies in African and Caribbean Literature. Cambridge, UK: Cambridge University Press, 1990.

Killam, G. D. "Chinua Achebe's Novels." *Sewanee Review* 79 (1971): 514–541.

Lindfors, Bernth. *Folklore in Nigerian Literature.* New York: Africana Press, 1973.

Muoneke, Romanus Okey. *Art, Rebellion, and Redemption: A Reading of the Novels of Chinua Achebe.* New York: Peter Lang, 1994.

Njoku, Benedict Chiaka. *Four Novels of Chinua Achebe: A Critical Study.* New York: Peter Lang, 1984.

Ogbaa, Kalu. *Gods, Oracles, and Divinations: Folkways in Chinua Achebe's Novels.* Trenton, NJ: Africa World Press, 1992.

Ojinmah, Umelo. *Chinua Achebe: New Perspectives.* Ibadan, Nigeria: Spectrum, 1991.

Achebe's Literature for Children

While literary works intended for adults often engage political and social issues directly, the purpose of children's literature is fundamentally different. Children's literature deals with personal issues, often focusing on a single character—usually a child, like the intended reader, or sometimes animals or other fantastic beings. The literary purpose of this construction is to create identification between reader and character. The social purpose of children's literature is to introduce children to the values and rules of their culture. The figure of the mother as storyteller, so common in Chinua Achebe's novels, performs this task for the children of the Ibo.

The stories mothers tell about animals in the forest communicate a society's values. When a nation is under colonial rule, however, when its schools and libraries are administered from the outside, the values and rules will be those, not of the children's own culture, but of the colonizer. To create a distinct national identity, children must have a literature that addresses their own concerns. In the 1960s Achebe's committment to the task of nation building in Nigeria included the creation of a Nigerian children's literature.

His first children's novel was *Chike and the River,* in 1966. Young Chike goes from his village to town for school; he finds many of his fellow students dishonest or foolish. Chike's fondest wish is to take a boat across the Niger River, but as soon as he gets the money to do so, he loses it. Chike earns the money again, but on the trip he ends up getting stranded overnight. He encounters a gang of robbers and helps the police apprehend them. He becomes famous for this courageous act, and the store owner who was robbed volunteers to pay for Chike's education. His virtue is rewarded.

Soon after, Achebe and his friend Christopher Okigbo founded the Citadel Press, dedicated to publishing African children's literature. The first manuscript they received was entitled "How the Dog Was Domesticated." The story charmed Achebe, who began to edit it. He ended up coauthoring the story, which became *How the Leopard Got His Claws.*

In the tale the leopard, the king of the animals, proposes that the animals build a shelter. Most agree with this plan, except for the dog, who already has a cave, and the duck. The others complete the building, but when a heavy rain drives the dog from his cave, he goes to the communal shelter and chases everyone out. The leopard encourages the other animals to fight the dog, but they refuse and hail the dog as their new leader. The leopard finds a blacksmith, who makes him a set of fearsome teeth and claws. Borrowing a voice from the thunder, the leopard defeats the dog, pulls down the communal dwelling, and announces that he will "rule the forest with terror" from that day forward. The dog seeks protection from humans, and the animals are enemies still.

Citadel Press never got off the ground, cut short by the death of Christopher Okigbo in the Biafran War, but *How the Leopard Got His Claws* was eventually published elsewhere, and Achebe continued to write for children.

An Ibo sculptor and his assistant create masks and elaborate carvings from tree trunks harvested from the nearby forest. Achebe's children's books celebrate the everyday life of his people and serve as valuable documents rendering and passing on the mores and values of his culture. Storytelling is a treasured and exalted art among the Ibo.

The Flute and *The Drum,* which retell traditional Ibo stories, were published in 1977. In *The Flute* a boy forgets his flute on the farm and begs for permission to go back for it. His mother refuses, saying he would disturb the spirits who rule at night. The boy made this flute himself, so he disobeys and goes anyway. At the farm he encounters the king of the spirits, who chastises the boy for disobedience but hails him for bravery, because both qualities are important.

In *The Drum* a tortoise wanders into the land of the spirits and is given a gift, a drum that when it is beaten makes food. The tortoise takes it back to the other animals and sets himself up as king, but in the preparations for his coronation, the drum is beaten too hard and breaks. The tortoise then goes in search of another drum from the spirits. The new drum gives out punishments, not food, but the tortoise decides that if the animals were willing to share his bounty, they should also share his suffering.

Achebe has written many kinds of children's stories, but all make similar ethical points. He may well have fulfilled his goal of giving African children a literature of their own.

SOURCES FOR FURTHER STUDY

Dow, Miriam. "A Postcolonial Child: Achebe's Chike at the Crossroads." *Children's Literature Association Quarterly* 22, no. 4 (winter 1997/1998): 160–165.

Joseph, Michael Scott. "A Pre-Modernist Reading of 'The Drum': Chinua Achebe and the Theme of Eternal Return." *Ariel* 28, no. 1 (January 1997): 149–166.

THINGS FALL APART

Genre: Novel
Subgenre: Realistic fiction
Published: Nigeria, 1958
Time period: About 1880 to 1900
Setting: Umuofia, an Ibo village in eastern Nigeria

Themes and Issues. The major theme in *Things Fall Apart* concerns the effects of the colonial encounter on a traditional animist African village. Umuofia is not a small, ignorant place waiting patiently for the blessings of Western civilization; it is a fully formed community with a coherent, if brutal, philosophical and social structure. Okonkwo believes in the old ways, which he has mastered. He submits to the will of the elders and the gods but not to those weaker than he. His adherence to tradition, which could also be seen as an inability to understand and adapt to the changing world, is his tragic flaw and leads to his fall in this clearly tragic story.

The Plot. Okonkwo, a noble warrior of the Ibo tribe, has three wives and is a leader in the village of Umuofia. His father was lazy and improvident and left his children nothing, so Okonkwo earned his reputation through wrestling, war, and the wealth he worked so hard to accumulate. At the same time he is brusque, almost rude, to those less successful than he and hates any sign of weakness or femininity.

The wife of one of the village residents is killed in a neighboring village. Instead of going to war, Umuofia demands tribute: a girl, to replace the murdered woman, and a boy, as a

fine. The boy, Ikemefuna, comes to live at Okonkwo's house, where he stays for several years. Okonkwo likes him, thinking him a better son than his own son, Nwoye. Ikemefuna befriends Nwoye, becomes beloved in the family, and eventually calls Okonkwo father.

In Achebe's *Things Fall Apart,* a price is placed on human life. A boy and girl are ceded to Okonkwo's community in exchange for a wrongful death suffered at the hands of a rival village. Threatened by and spurning the power of the feminine, Okonkwo takes in the boy, Ikemefuna. Though the child appears to be seamlessly integrated into his new family, there are forces at work in the novel that destroy the harmonious adoption. Okonkwo's pride and easily threatened masculinity impel him to join the group of vigilantes who kill Ikemefuna. Thus the rigidity of custom and gender roles conspires in the novel to leave Okonkwo with nothing but an inheritance of guilt.

After three years an oracle declares that Ikemefuna must die. An elder member of the tribe tells Okonkwo to have no part in his death: since the boy calls him father, it would be an abomination. Okonkwo, scared of being thought weak, goes with the party that kills Ikemefuna. Okonkwo is very upset and stops eating for several days in grief for the boy. Nwoye, though he has been told that Ikemefuna has returned to his people, knows the truth.

Life in the village goes on: marriages, feasts, funerals. At one funeral Okonkwo's gun accidentally discharges and kills the son of the deceased. Banished from the tribe for seven years, Okonkwo moves his wife and children to Mbanta, the home of his mother's kinsmen, where he is well received. He is mortified, however, that he has been thrown back on his female connections. The Ibo have a saying, "*Nneka* (mother) is supreme." Okonkwo, loathing weakness and femininity, does not believe the saying, and although he prospers in Mbanta, he is not happy there.

Okonkwo's friend Obierika visits Mbanta several times to bring him news. There has been a massacre in Abame because the villagers killed a white messenger on the order of their oracle. Soldiers surrounded the market and attempted to kill everyone. A few escaped to Umuofia to tell the tale. In Umuofia an Englishman has arrived and built a Christian church. The elders think it is a bad sign, but they do not think it is a serious threat and allow it because the Englishman's only followers are rejects from the tribe. Obierika shares this news with Okonkwo because Nwoye, his son, is among the Christians. The missionaries

Like Achebe's 1958 novel, *Things Fall Apart,* this 1893 illustration captures the inherent paradox of colonialism. While in theory the foreign powers attempted to enlighten and improve the lives of Africans, they often managed only to dehumanize them.

have also been to Mbanta, and Nwoye has run away to join them. Nwoye has never forgiven his father for the murder of Ikemefuna, and this new religion, without oracles and sacrifices, appeals to him.

The Christian leader, Mr. Brown, does everything he can to avoid provoking the anger of the clan. He visits respected leaders and talks with them about their gods and God. In this way he protects his converts from their own families. When one fanatical convert kills the sacred python of the tribe and dies while doing so, the tribe assumes that the gods can fight for themselves and the Christians can be left alone.

Okonkwo returns to Umuofia to find that not only the church but the British government is now active in the town. He is angry, but many in the town approve: they now have a trading post, and their palm oil, an expensive commodity, brings in much money.

When Mr. Brown returns to England, he is replaced by the Reverend James Smith, who sees the world as divided into black and white and determines to wipe out the black— Umuofia and its traditional beliefs, Okonkwo's world. Smith protects people who actively insult the clan. Eventually, the *egwugwu*, human manifestations of ancient tribal spirits, attack the church and burn it to the ground.

The minister invokes the help of the British authorities, who lure the village leaders— including Okonkwo—into a meeting, where they are arrested and briefly imprisoned. A village meeting to discuss the situation is disturbed by British messengers; Okonkwo shoots and kills one. The others are allowed to escape and report the crime. When the district commissioner comes to arrest Okonkwo, he finds that Okonkwo has already committed suicide. The leaders of Umuofia ask for British help in burying the dead man; a taboo prevents them from handling a suicide. The district commissioner thinks Okonkwo's case is interesting and plans to mention it in his book, *The Pacification of the Primitive Tribes of the Lower Niger.*

Analysis. The title of the novel comes from William Butler Yeats's poem "The Second Coming," an apocalyptic vision of the destruction of the world. It is fitting as a title for the destruction of this society.

The real power of *Things Fall Apart*, Achebe's first and still most widely read novel, is its articulate and well-defined picture of a precolonial African society. Umuofia is never quaint or merely colorful; though Achebe wrote the novel in English, not Ibo, the villagers' language is full of proverbs and traditional wisdom.

Okonkwo is not really representative of his society; his nervous protection of his reputation makes him too stiff and angry to fit in. Nonetheless, as a man worthy of respect, he embodies the values of his society. Okonkwo's resistance to European culture should not be seen as prescient. He does not know that it will mean the end of the old ways, and he would resist any other outside force just as strongly. As it turns out, of course, the new European religion and government do destroy his society.

SOURCES FOR FURTHER STUDY

Iyasere, Solomon O. *Understanding "Things Fall Apart": Selected Essays and Criticism.* Troy, NY: Whitson, 1998.

Ogbaa, Kalu. *Understanding "Things Fall Apart": A Student Casebook to Issues, Sources, and Historical Documents.* Westport, CT: Greenwood Press, 1999.

NO LONGER AT EASE

Genre: Novel
Subgenre: Realistic fiction
Published: Nigeria, 1960
Time period: 1956–1957
Setting: Lagos and Umuofia, Nigeria

Themes and Issues. The major theme of *No Longer at Ease* is the conflict between tradition and modernity. On the one hand, the protagonist, Obi Okonkwo, is a creation of his people, his village, and his family. They have raised him and funded his education, and they expect him to come back and contribute to the community. On the other hand, he is just as much a product of the English colonial system. He is a Christian, has been educated in England, and knows English literature. He sees himself as an individual, not as a representative of his race or his village. Corruption is

One of Chinua Achebe's most profound inspirations has been the Ibo oral tradition, which he has sought to represent in both his language and his content. The use of proverbs and folktales points to a tradition of spoken rather than written literature and to the world Achebe inhabited as a child.

At the same time, he has been profoundly influenced by the European literary tradition, particularly the British tradition. In *Home and Exile* he explains how many of his schoolmates chafed under rules that required them to read novels from the school library; he never found this restriction to be a problem. Achebe particularly cites Robert Louis Stevenson, Jonathan Swift, and Walter Scott, among others, as authors whose work "entranced" him; he described their fiction as "so different from the stories of my home and childhood." This love of stories and storytelling has traveled with him throughout his life.

Inspirations can be very specific events, in turn prompting very specific responses. One incident in Achebe's college career involved the effort of a well-meaning teacher to give his Nigerian students a text they could identify with, as opposed to the kind of British literature they were usually taught. The book in question was Joyce Cary's *Mister Johnson,* a critique of British colonialism in Nigeria. Cary's shallow and caricatured representations of Achebe's countrymen, legend has it, inspired Achebe to write a novel that would replace these colonialist stereotypes with fully formed, intelligent native characters. This novel became *Things Fall Apart.* (More recently Achebe has cast some doubt upon this tale of inspiration. Though he acknowledges its basic truth, he complicates his reasoning in *Home and Exile.*)

another major theme in the novel. Obi works in a system in which corruption is taken for granted but is seen as the specific failing of the native population. Obi is strong enough to resist it for a long time, but when he is at his weakest, he succumbs and pays the price.

The Plot. As the novel opens, Obi Okonkwo is standing trial for bribery. The judge chastises him and wonders why a young man of such promise has gone wrong. Obi, the grandson of the protagonist of *Things Fall Apart,* is indeed a young man of promise. He has been reared as a Christian (his father is Nwoye, Okonkwo's Christian son), and the people of his village have raised money for him to attend school in England. There, rather than train to become a doctor or lawyer or enter some profession that would help the people who are paying his way, he chooses to study English literature.

On his return to Nigeria, he meets a young woman on the boat who has also been studying in England, a nurse named Clara. She is from a village near his own and is, like him, Ibo. When he returns to Nigeria, he obtains a post in the civil service judging scholarship applications for other young people to study abroad. It is a well-paying job, and he immediately acquires an apartment in a largely European neighborhood, a car, and servants. He also begins dating Clara. Their relationship becomes serious, and over the protestations of his friends, he asks her to marry him. She declines, telling him that although she loves him, she is an *osu*: one of her ancestors was given as a gift to the gods, and his line is cursed in Ibo society. He does not care and presses her to marry him.

Meanwhile, Obi's financial situation is growing worse by the day. Because he is in a good position, he is expected to show generosity, as well as

The imposing male figure in Willie Birch's 2000 work *The Grand Marshals* suggests the tortured Obi in Achebe's 1960 novel, *No Longer at Ease.* The lure of wealth and authority turned some leaders away from once noble intentions and idealistic hopes of improving the lives of their fellow citizens. Obi cannot synthesize the competing influences in his life. The tradition of his village and the advancement afforded him by his Western education clash, and the resultant unresolved tensions they engender eventually lead to his downfall.

make a good public showing as a wealthy man. He must repay his townspeople for the money they have spent on him, he has taxes and insurance fees to pay, and he is also sending money to his parents. At one point, coming up short, he borrows money from Clara to pay his insurance.

At the same time his job, which permits him to determine scholarship recipients, also makes

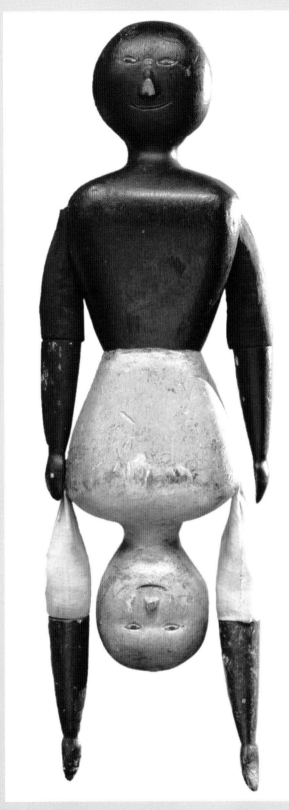

By employing Western or colonialist means of self-advancement, Obi grows dangerously out of touch with his native origins in Achebe's *No Longer at Ease.* In this sense, the novel becomes a cautionary tale and its protagonist a symbol of modern Nigeria, where an uneasy balance exists between two sources of influence and guidance, two heads doing the thinking for one national body. This tenuous union is embodied by an anonymous arist's *Topsy-Turvy Doll.*

him subject to bribery. Several people come forward: men offer him money, girls offer him sexual favors, all in exchange for preferential treatment in the scholarship process. He disdainfully dismisses all offers, knowing the reputation native Nigerian officials have as corrupt, particularly in the eyes of the British colonial service.

Eventually he receives a letter from his father telling him that he must come home to discuss something important. Obi knows that his father must have heard of his relationship with Clara, the *osu.* Even though he cannot afford a visit home, he takes two weeks' leave and returns to Umuofia. Before he goes, Clara tries to break off their engagement. At home his father confronts him about Clara, and Obi points out that their family is Christian and should not be held by the heathen traditions of their ancestors. This argument almost convinces his father. Then Obi speaks with his mother, who is dying. She is more traditional than his father, closer to the old Ibo ways. His mother tells him that, if he must marry this girl, to wait until she dies. If he does not, she will kill herself.

Obi returns to Lagos and breaks up with Clara, who is pregnant. She flatly refuses to marry him. Now he needs to come up with money for an abortion, as well as all his other expenses. He borrows money from a politician he knows, but the abortion does not go well, and Clara is hospitalized for several weeks. In the meantime his mother dies, and Obi cannot afford to go home for the funeral. The members of the Umuofia community in Lagos come to offer their condolences and, while there, point out that Obi's father also skipped his own father's funeral, a sign of disrespect.

With all these difficult circumstances hitting him at once, the one thing Obi can do something about is his financial situation. Since he has lost both his mother and his fiancée, he no longer cares about himself or his reputation and so gives in to the prevailing atmosphere of corruption. He accepts first one bribe, then others. He is careful to accept bribes only from qualified applicants, so no inappropriate applicants get through. Nevertheless, he is caught in a sting operation and arrested for bribery, the trial for which began the novel.

Analysis: Obi Okonkwo, like his grandfather, is essentially a tragic figure. He should have everything he needs: money, education, intelligence, and even integrity. Just as his grandfather was successful in Ibo society, Obi is successful in modern Nigerian society. The feeling of success ultimately eludes him because there are so many calls on his allegiance and resources. As the various ropes tighten around Obi—family, community, love, money, the responsibility of the educated native to represent his race to the English colonial power structure—the reader is inclined to believe, as Obi does, that he will find a way out of his various predicaments, but the structures in which he functions are too rigid to give him any freedom of movement, and he meets his inevitable tragic end. No one force can be said to be truly responsible for his fate, but in combination they are fatal.

SOURCES FOR FURTHER STUDY

Carroll, David. *Chinua Achebe: Novelist, Poet, Critic.* London: Macmillan, 1980. Reprint, 1990. See especially chapter 3, "No Longer at Ease."

Gikandi, Simon. *Reading Chinua Achebe: Language and Ideology in Fiction.* Studies in African Literature. Portsmouth, NH: Heinemann, 1991. See especially chapter 4, "Writing in the Marginal Space."

NOVELS

1958 Things Fall Apart
1960 No Longer at Ease
1964 Arrow of God
1966 A Man of the People
1987 Anthills of the Savannah

SHORT STORY COLLECTIONS

1962 The Sacrificial Egg and Other Stories
1972 Girls at War and Other Stories
1985 African Short Stories (edited with C. L. Innes)
1992 The Heinemann Book of Contemporary African Short Stories (edited with C. L. Innes)

POEMS

1971 Beware Soul Brother and Other Poems (reprinted in 1973 as Christmas in Biafra and Other Poems)
1978 Don't Let Him Die: An Anthology of Memorial Poems for Christopher Okigbo (1932–1967) (edited with Dubem Okafor)
1982 Aka Weta: Egwu agulu-agu egwu edeluede (edited with Obiora Udechukwu)
1997 Another Africa (with photographs by Robert Lyons)

CHILDREN'S STORIES

1966 Chike and the River
1973 How the Leopard Got His Claws (with John Iroaganachi)
1977 The Drum
1977 The Flute

NONFICTION

1971 The Insider: Stories of War and Peace from Nigeria (editor)
1975 Morning Yet on Creation Day: Essays
1983 The Trouble with Nigeria
1986 The World of the Ogbanje
1988 Hopes and Impediments: Selected Essays, 1965–1987
1988 The University and the Leadership Factor in Nigerian Politics
1989 A Tribute to James Baldwin
1990 Beyond Hunger in Africa: Conventional Wisdom and an African Vision (editor)
2000 Home and Exile

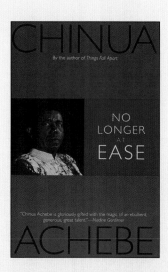

ARROW OF GOD (1964). Set in the 1920s, well after the British colonial presence had been established in Nigeria, *Arrow of God* tells the story of Ezelulu, the chief priest of the god Ulu. Ulu is the patron deity of the Ibo village in which the story is set, and so Ezelulu is a very important person in the life of the village, responsible for its many communal rituals. Ezelulu, as stubbornly traditional as Okonkwo in *Things Fall Apart,* risks his power in trying to prevent his village from going to war with a nearby village, a position that makes him a hero to the British colonizers but costs him the allegiance of his own people.

When the British attempt to elevate him to village chieftain, a position Ezelulu refuses, the real nature of the colonial relationship is revealed in the angry words of the British administrator Clarke: "A witch doctor making a fool of the British Administration in public!" Ezelulu discovers, however, that despite acting according to principle and tradition in both cases, he has lost the faith of his village and of the new colonial administration. He descends into madness.

The narrative structure of *Arrow of God* is similar to that of *Things Fall Apart,* but Ezelulu's position and his supernatural power make his

Fractured perspectives and the multiplicity of identity are strong underpinnings in Achebe's work. In *Anthills of the Savannah,* the three boyhood friends represent the competing voices, each with its own notion of the past and possible future direction of the fictional African nation, Kangan, which stands for Achebe's Nigeria. Beatrice is an indirect victim of their split perspectives. When the three characters look to their fellow citizens, are they seeing the true individual or versions of the self, the shadows and doppelgängers that form the subject of Hughie Lee-Smith's 1997 oil-on-canvas *Silhouette and Shadow*?

fall even more tragic than Okonkwo's, in that it reveals not only the conflict between the indigenous population and the European colonizers but also the crisis within indigenous society itself and the failure of the traditional social structures to demand allegiance.

ANTHILLS OF THE SAVANNAH (1987).

Set in the fictional African country of Kangan, a thinly veiled Nigeria, *Anthills of the Savannah* tells the story of the declining days of the regime of Sam, the head of state, a general who has nodded to democracy by appointing a civilian cabinet. One of his cabinet members is his friend Christopher Oriko, the minister for information, who is under suspicion as the novel begins because, as an old friend of His Excellency, he has suggested that the ruler might be making political mistakes. The story focuses on Chris; his girlfriend, Beatrice, a bureaucrat in the Ministry of Finance; and their friend Ikem Osodi, a newspaper editor critical of the government, though Sam is a constant presence in their consideration and conversations.

The novel has several narrators, each giving his or her own perspective on the events of the story. This strategy produces several effects. One is a sense of discomfort caused by the rapidly shifting narrative, a sense that the truth is not necessarily even graspable. Another is the related observation that each character may have access to some part of the truth, but they cannot all be right.

Anthills of the Savannah chronicles the descent into paranoia and assassination that accompanies the corruption of state power. His Excellency has been told not to trust his old school friends, Chris and Ikem, because they will never treat him with the appropriate respect. Ikem's journalistic freedom, which Ikem insists upon, is seen by Sam as a threat to his power. To make things worse, Ikem is a native of a section of the country in which His Excellency's support is weak, a weakness Sam (correctly, as it turns out) blames on Ikem.

Obi (right), an Ibo leader from Onitsha, a city in eastern Nigeria on the banks of the Niger River, accepts the traditional greeting from one of his followers, kneeling and placing the head on the ground. The ruler is flanked by his prime minister. Achebe's *Anthills of the Savannah* centers on issues of authority and is imbued with layers of political complexity. Not only is the novel informed by a conflict among Africans for power, but the specter of colonial control is a constant presence, hanging in the background. In such a world, clarity is often compromised, a state Achebe enacts in the plurality of voices and perspectives he presents, each narrator seemingly holding a piece of an elusive truth.

Meanwhile, Beatrice is invited to dinner by the head of state, where she meets a number of people. Understanding that the official cabinet is a sham and that her fellow guests are Sam's real advisers, she begins to fear for Chris.

As minister of information, Chris is forced to suspend Ikem from his position shortly before he is scheduled to give a talk at the National University. At that talk Ikem criticizes the corruption and inefficiency of the government and accuses the students of merely wanting a turn at the trough instead of real reform. He also criticizes the megalomania of Sam, who is considering putting his own head on the nation's currency. Ikem observes that "any President foolish enough to put his head on a coin is inciting people to take it off," a statement that is interpreted by his pro-government replacement as advocating regicide. Soon the university is closed down, and Ikem is murdered by security forces.

Chris and Beatrice realize the danger they are in, and Chris goes into hiding. He is spirited out of the capital by bus, accompanied by a student leader. At a bus stop far into Abazon, they hear that His Excellency has been kidnapped and murdered, not by reformist forces but by one of his own cabinet ministers. In the public celebration on the street, a drunken policeman tries to rape a young girl. Chris, no longer frightened, steps forward to stop him and is killed. Several months later, Ikem's girlfriend gives birth to his daughter. She is given a boy's name, Amaechina, a name meaning "may the path never close." The novel ends with the women (and a few men) creating a small community, heading toward a hopeful future.

Anthills is based loosely on the Nigerian coup of 1985, though it was begun much earlier. It concerns many of the issues Achebe had addressed throughout his career, particularly that of political corruption in the African states. It is a personal story of three boyhood friends who as a group embody the fate of the nation. As Beatrice observes, "all three of you are incredibly conceited. The story of this country, as far as you are concerned, is the story of the three of you." In making the long-standing connections between the friends personal rather than just political, Achebe hints at the long history of regional and ethnic conflict plaguing the state, and by removing all three, he allows for a new beginning.

A MAN OF THE PEOPLE (1966). *A Man of the People* is one of Achebe's several novels that directly address political corruption in contemporary postcolonial Africa. Its protagonist, Odili, a schoolteacher, narrates the novel. Use of first-person narration allows the reader to understand Odili in a way one often cannot understand other Achebe protagonists. Odili's

The use of the first person in Achebe's *A Man of the People* lends immediacy to the novel and provides a powerful insight into character usually denied the writer's other protagonists. The device allows Achebe to focus on the individual, suggested here by Sidney Goodman's 1988 charcoal-and-pastel-on-paper *Study for Political Prisoner* (Pennsylvania Academy of Fine Arts, Philadelphia). Odili's "I" is a lone voice powerless and unheard against the clamoring of the vast and corrupt political machine that surrounds him.

regular recourse to cliché and glib answers to complex questions clearly marks the character as human and fallible.

The focus of the novel is Odili's relationship with his former teacher, M. A. Nanga. Nanga has become a popular politician and earned posts in the national government, both in parliament and as the minister of culture. Odili, initially warm toward Nanga, begins to see the corruption underneath the charming exterior. Idealistically, he decides to challenge Nanga for his parliamentary seat. Odili attempts to reach out to the people, but doing so renders him part of the system he is attempting to defeat. After electoral humiliation and physical attack, Odili accepts that the system is too corrupt for him to penetrate. Nanga's ill-gotten victory, however, is soon moot: he and the rest of the sitting government are overthrown in a coup d'etat, a plot device that might seem somewhat contrived except for its sad predictability in the political life of Nigeria. (Achebe was quite prescient: *A Man of the People* was published as the government was ousted, civil war loomed, and Achebe was displaced from Lagos back to his native district. Though the author should not be confused with his narrator, Odili's characterization of the "fat-dripping, gummy, eat-and-let-eat regime just ended" is probably close to Achebe's own.)

Resources

As of 2002 none of Achebe's novels had been made into films—an unsurprising fact, given their often tragic tone. There are, however, some excellent introductions to his work and thought available on video and the Internet.

Chinua Achebe. In 1994 the television journalist Bill Moyers interviewed Achebe about the West's perception of Africa and the responsibility of the African storyteller to his people. This interview, titled *Chinua Achebe,* was produced and directed by Gail Pellett (Films for the Humanities and Sciences).

Chinua Achebe: African Literature as Celebration. Directed by Daniel Wiles (Films for the Humanities and Sciences, 1999), this is a recording of a lecture in which Achebe discusses the explosion of literature in Nigeria and other African countries during the latter half of the twentieth century.

Chinua Achebe: Africa's Voice. This video, written and directed by David Akinde (Trident Communications, 1999), includes a detailed analysis of *Things Fall Apart.* The video features interviews with Achebe and other scholars of African literature. The section on Ibo oral culture and philosophy is particularly useful.

Web Sites. Of the Internet sites on Achebe and his work, one of the most thorough is the Postcolonial Web, moderated by the National University of Singapore. It features special sections on Africa, Nigeria, and Achebe's life and works, including several critical studies of the novels (http://www.scholars.nus.edu.sg/landow/post/achebe.html). Also interesting are the introductory materials on Achebe at Pegasos, a Finnish literature resource site (http://www.kirjasto.sci.fi/achebe.htm).

MARY E. DONNELLY

Isabel Allende

BORN: August 2, 1942, Lima, Peru

IDENTIFICATION: Chilean novelist who became the first female writer from Latin America to achieve international acclaim for her novels, which combine magic realism and political criticism.

SIGNIFICANCE: A voluntary exile from her native Chile, Isabel Allende has written eight novels and two collections of short stories; most of her work has been translated from her original Spanish into a great many other languages. Her first novel, *The House of the Spirits* (1982), set the tone for her later works, all of which, in presenting resourceful and powerful women, run counter to the Latin literary tradition of portraying women as docile or subservient. Allende's works, centered around dynamic female protagonists, usually incorporate themes from history or from her own life, even including the early death of her daughter. Some of her novels and stories have been adapted for film and the stage.

The Writer's Life

On August 2, 1942, Isabel Allende was born to Tomás Allende and Francisca Llona, in Lima, Peru, where her father was stationed as a diplomat. Her parents' marriage ended in annulment when she was only three years old (Chile did not allow divorce at that time). Her mother soon after returned to Chile with her three children, and Isabel spent the next eight years at her grandparents' house in Santiago.

Childhood. Allende's grandparents were a major influence in her life. Her grandmother loved the supernatural and passed this fascination on to the young girl. Meanwhile, her grandfather was an avid reader and storyteller who routinely read massive works such as the Bible or the *Encyclopaedia Britannica*. Allende grew up listening to the tales of both her grandparents, and this environment served as the foundation for her later works. She soon began to develop her own stories and often regaled her family with these tales.

Allende grew up among the wealthy and powerful of Chile. It was a culture that was very traditional and emphasized the dominance of men and the subservience of women. Honor and family were more important than individual happiness or love. Allende resented the confines and rigidity of Chilean culture, especially the role it assigned to women.

In 1953 her mother married Ramón Huidobro, who was also a diplomat. During the next five years Allende lived first in Bolivia and then in Lebanon. In both places she attended exclusive private schools that conducted lessons in English. This experience exposed her to non-Hispanic cultures and introduced her to European literary influences. In 1958 the dangers presented by the civil war in Lebanon led her parents to send Allende and her two brothers back to Chile.

Marriage. Upon her return to Chile, Allende again lived with her grandparents. She also completed her education. At age 15 she met her future husband, Miguel Frias, who was an Anglo-Chilean engineering student at the time. Although women were not expected to have careers in Chile in the 1950s and 1960s, after she fin-

About a year old, Isabel Allende rests a hand on her mother's shoulder and looks into the distance. The young Francisca Llona Barros is described in Allende's *Paula* as "a sensitive girl," but she looks formidable as she cradles Francisco, born in 1943 and the second of her three children with Tomás Allende. Allende has said, "My mother is the longest love affair of my life. We have never cut the umbilical cord." Of her father, who soon vanished from their lives, Allende said, "I scarcely remember him at all; I must have closed him into some sealed compartment of my heart."

ished school, Allende went to work for the Chilean Food and Agriculture Organization. In 1962 she married Miguel, and a year later a daughter, Paula, was born. After a year traveling throughout Europe with her husband and family, Allende returned to Chile, where she gave birth to a son, Nicolás, in 1966.

The Fledgling Writer. After Nicolás was born, Allende decided to utilize her talents and experiences and embark on a career as a writer. She wanted to express her unhappiness with the nature of Chilean society. Allende joined the editorial board of the feminist journal *Paula* and began to write a regular column entitled "The Impertinents," which combined humor and radical critiques of society and politics.

Her work was very well received and opened the door to a variety of other opportunities. For instance, in 1970 she developed programming for two television stations in Santiago, Chile. Meanwhile, she wrote a play and several children's stories and in 1973 began writing for the children's magazine *Mampato*.

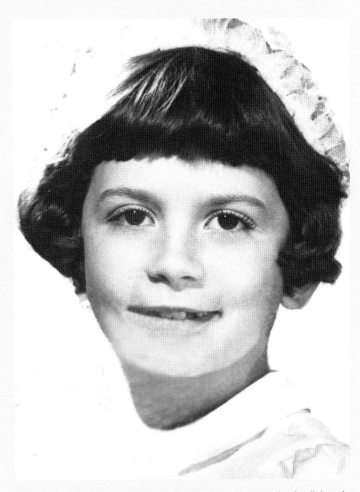

Allende, dressed for First Communion in 1950. She was the family's only child to be born in a hospital, and Allende says her mother panicked when the staff kept the two of them apart. So Allende's mother and grandmother discreetly and hastily kidnapped the baby. "They didn't have time to dwell on details—they just grabbed the first infant they saw and ran: me. That explains a lot of things. . . . Maybe I'm not me; maybe I'm taking the place that legitimately belongs to another little girl."

Political Turmoil. Allende's uncle, Salvador Allende, a socialist, who was vehemently opposed by the nation's powerful military, was elected president of Chile in 1970. On September 11, 1973, with the support of the United States, the Chilean military, led by General Augusto Pinochet, overthrew Allende's elected government and assassinated Allende.

Although she faced political persecution, Allende voiced opposition to the government through her writings. Most of the rest of her family fled from Chile to avoid repression, but Allende, determined to fight the military regime, stayed behind and became involved in the resistance movement against the Pinochet dictatorship. However, with thousands arrested

and the regime becoming more brutal, she realized that she could not safely remain in Chile with her family. In 1975 she went into exile in Venezuela with her husband and children.

Life in exile was difficult. The family had little money, and Allende felt isolated from both her relatives and her native country. She settled in Caracas, Venezuela, with her husband and children and went to work for the city's main newspaper, *El Nacional*. By 1978 the strain of exile and an increasing number of marital problems led Allende to temporarily leave her husband and move to Spain, but she returned after only a few months and continued to work as a journalist. She also accepted an administrative position with Marroco College in Caracas.

HIGHLIGHTS IN ALLENDE'S LIFE

1942   Isabel Allende is born on August 2 in Lima, Peru.

1945   Her parents divorce.

1953–1958 Allende's mother and new stepfather move the family to Bolivia and then Lebanon.

1962   Allende marries Miguel Frias.

1963   Daughter, Paula, is born.

1966   Son, Nicolás, is born.

1967–1974 Allende becomes a journalist; works for a number of journals and news organizations, including television stations.

1973   Her uncle, Salvador Allende, the Chilean president, is overthrown in a military coup.

1975   Allende flees to Venezuela, where she becomes a newspaper columnist.

1981   Writes a lengthy letter to her dying grandfather, which later becomes the basis for *The House of the Spirits*.

1982   Publishes her first novel, *The House of the Spirits*.

1985   *The House of the Spirits* is translated into English; Allende moves to the United States to teach writing at several colleges and universities.

1987   Divorces Frias.

1988   Marries Willie Gordon; moves to San Rafael, California; publishes a collection of short stories, *The Stories of Eva Luna*, which is adapted for the stage.

1992   Daughter, Paula, dies of porphyria.

1993   *The House of the Spirits* is adapted for the stage in London and for the screen.

1994   Allende publishes *Paula*, a book inspired by the death of her daughter.

1996   Receives Critics' Choice Award in the United States.

1999   Receives the Dorothy and Lillian Gish Prize; publishes *Daughter of Fortune*.

Literary Breakthrough. In 1981 Allende received news that her grandfather, now 99 years old, was dying. In response she began to compose a lengthy letter to him in which she expressed her feelings, both positive and negative, about their family. She was deeply upset that she could not return to Chile to be with him. Before she completed the letter, he died. As a tribute to her grandfather, Allende decided to use the note as the basis of a new novel. The resultant book, *The House of the Spirits,* was published in 1982.

A fashionable woman and her slightly stodgy-looking in-law: the writer's mother poses with the president of Chile in 1972. Salvador Allende, Isabel's uncle, had helped found the country's Socialist Party in 1933; almost forty years later a three-way election race made him the country's first Marxist president. With just 36% of the vote behind him, he challenged U.S. companies, raised wages, froze prices, and moved to take over big agricultural estates. The year after this photograph was taken, a coup would leave him dead and begin seventeen years of dictatorship. His tragedy became central to Allende's first novel, *The House of the Spirits.*

Shadows (1984) and *Eva Luna* (1987). As a result of her success in writing fiction, Allende stopped writing for *El Nacional* and concentrated on novels and short stories.

Family Struggles. Although Allende and her husband had been able temporarily to repair their marriage, the death of Allende's grandfather and Allende's newfound literary success increased tensions between the couple, and in 1987 the two were divorced. Allende left Venezuela to give lectures on her work and to teach writing at a number of American colleges and universities. While in the United States, Allende met William "Willie" Gordon, an American lawyer. The two fell in love and were married on July 17, 1988.

In 1990, extremely happy with her new husband, Allende received welcome news from her homeland. The military dictatorship finally decided to allow free elections in Chile. After Patricio Aylwin became the first democratically elected president in 17 years, Allende returned to Chile to visit and to receive several literary awards from her native country.

Allende with her second husband, Willie Gordon of the United States, in the home of poet Pablo Neruda on Isla Negra, Chile. Early in their marriage she wrote the novel *The Infinite Plan* as a tribute to Gordon. A critic doubted "that so many things could have occurred in one lifetime," Allende recalls. "The truth was that actually I had to leave parts out because the real story seemed exaggerated."

Allende drew on her own family's history and the stories told to her as a child to create this novel, which traces the rise of several generations of an imaginary Chilean family. Written in Spanish, the book gained international praise and was translated into dozens of languages, bringing immediate fame to Allende. Unfortunately, even though her novel was named the book of the year in Chile, Allende was unable to return to her homeland because of her political differences with the military regime. She followed the success of her first novel with several works that were also widely translated, including *Of Love and*

Just as it seemed that Allende's success in her private life was beginning to match her success as a writer, tragedy struck. Her daughter, Paula, fell into a coma, which was caused by the rare disease porphyria. On December 6, 1992, Paula died. Allende expressed her feelings about her daughter's death through the novel *Paula* (1994). Her greatest commercial success in the United States came in 1999 with the publication of *Daughter of Fortune*. As of 2002 Allende has continued to write and enjoy widespread international acclaim.

The Writer's Work

Isabel Allende is best known for her novels, although she has also written short stories and plays. In addition, she has considerable experience as a journalist and has written a variety of children's works and humorous essays. The medium that she has consistently avoided is poetry. Her fiction is often historical in nature and centered around powerful female characters. The works usually offer a rich blend of politics, the supernatural, and strong character development.

Unique Qualities. Although Allende's works are internationally known, she writes only in Spanish because of the complexity of her stories and her writing process. However, she has developed long relationships with her translators so that her stories are faithfully communicated to readers in other languages. Allende begins all of her novels on January 8, the date on which she began writing her first book, *The House of the Spirits*. In most of her works, the main characters are women, but in *The Infinite Plan* the main character is based on her husband Willie. Throughout her works Allende has consistently developed the theme that women can be independent, whether of their families or of the men in their lives.

Issues in Allende's Fiction. Many of Allende's works are written in a style known as magic realism. In this form of fiction, dreams

Allende in 1973, a TV personality and humorist. Her work has needled husbands, Don Juans, and machismo in general. That year her life, and her country's, was about to take a dangerous turn.

and visions allow characters to move between the spirit world and the real world. Allende's main characters often have magical powers, including the ability to go into deep trances and to disappear at will. In addition, within each work Allende often describes the same event from a variety of perspectives. For instance, men and women witnessing the same event may come away with very different interpretations; members of different generations also have conflicting memories. This complexity in life increases the complexity of her stories and allows Allende to explore the importance of gender and culture in people's perceptions of the world.

The importance of history and its continuing impact on the modern world forms one of the central themes in Allende's fiction. For instance, *The House of the Spirits* deals with several generations of a family and *Daughter of Fortune* is set during the California Gold Rush of 1849. The use of history complements Allende's magic realism by expanding the scope of the novels and reinforcing the distinctions between the real and spiritual world.

Allende's fiction is deeply political. It examines the importance of class and social standing in society and points out the manner in which people are treated differently on the basis of their status and power. In a variety of her works, including *The House of the Spirits* and *Of Love and Shadows,* Allende's principal characters are women who undergo transformations as they realize the unjust nature of dictatorial governments that are loosely based on the military regime in Chile. Many of Allende's works were published to add pressure for democracy and equal rights movements to build in Latin America. Her works can be seen as one component of the broad movement to end the dominance of the military in the region.

Characters in Allende's Fiction. Character development is central to all of Allende's fiction. While the majority of her protagonists are female, Allende has also demonstrated her ability to aptly portray strong male characters as well. Nonetheless, the most significant people in her fiction are heroines who overcome great obstacles. In *The House of the Spirits,* Clara del Valle, the matriarch of the powerful Trueba family, serves as the link between the world of magic and the real world. She also serves as the embodiment of the feminine spirit.

Key to the success of her political works is Allende's presentation of the complexity of her characters. For instance, although she bitterly opposed the supporters of the military regime in Chile, in her writing she very carefully presents the mixed emotions of Chilean conservatives toward the military coup. The patriarch of the Trueba clan in *The House of the Spirits,* the conservative Esteban Trueba, is forced to come to grips with the devastating impact of political repression on his own family. In *Of Love and Shadows,* Irene Beltran, a member of the wealthy class, becomes a staunch opponent of the government as a result of her investigation into the political persecutions carried out by the military regime.

Often the characters in Allende's work are drawn from her own life. Her first novel is a semiautobiographical work in which two characters, the matriarch and patriarch of the Trueba clan, are based on her grandparents. *Paula* is essentially a memoir of Allende's own life and her efforts to cope with the loss of her daughter. The male protagonist in *The Infinite Plan* is modeled on her husband Willie.

Allende's Literary Legacy. When Allende began her career, Latin American literature was dominated by men. Allende has been able to bring a different perspective on the culture and traditions of the region. Her works, a curious combination of the supernatural, politics, and feminism, echo the genre of magic realism.

Allende has specialized in highlighting the injustices of a region's society and especially the brutality of the military regime in Chile. These themes resonate with people throughout the world. Through her novels she has expanded the influence of Latin American literary traditions around the world. Within these traditions she has also increased the role and influence of female writers and feminist themes.

Her works have demonstrated that women can develop identities separate and independent from their relationships with men and even from their families.

BIBLIOGRAPHY

Agosin, Marjorie, and Celeste Kostopulos-Cooperman. *Tapestries of Hope, Threads of Love: The Arpillera Movement in Chile, 1974–1994.* Santa Fe: University of New Mexico Press, 1996.

Angulo, Maria-Elena. *Magic Realism: Social Context and Discourse.* Vol. 5. New York: Garland, 1997.

Cole, Melanie, Valerie Menard, Barbara Tidman, and Mitchell Lane. *Famous People of Latin Heritage.* Vol. 9. New York: Mitchell Lane, 1997.

Durix, Jean-Pierre. *Mimesis, Genres and Post-Colonial Discourse: Deconstructing Magic Realism.* New York: St. Martin's Press, 1998.

Fister, Barbara. *Third World Women's Literature: A Dictionary and Guide to Materials in English.* Westport, CT: Greenwood Press, 1995.

Hart, Patricia. *Narrative Magic in the Fiction of Isabel Allende.* Rutherford, NJ: Fairleigh Dickinson University Press, 1989.

Rodden, John, and Virginia Invernizzi. *Conversations with Isabel Allende.* Houston: University of Texas Press, 1999.

Rojas, Sonia Riquelme, and Edna Aguirre Rehbein, eds. *Critical Approaches to Isabel Allende's Novels.* New York: P. Lang, 1991.

Roman-Lagunas, Jorge. *The Chilean Novel: A Critical Study of Secondary Sources and a Bibliography.* Lanham, MD: Scarecrow Press, 1995.

Zamora, Lois Parkinson, and Wendy B. Faris, eds. *Magic Realism: Theory, History and Community.* Durham, NC: Duke University Press, 1995.

Spirituality means spirits in Allende's work, and both will often have a female face. The writer specializes in magic realism, with the everyday and the impossible overlapping. Allende calls it "a way of seeing in which there is space for the invisible forces that move the world: dreams, legends, myths, emotions, passion, history." The painting *Azazel's Revenge* by Catherine Porter-Brown may suggest much the same thing.

Reader's Guide to Major Works

THE HOUSE OF THE SPIRITS

Genre: Novel
Subgenre: Historical magic realism
Published: Barcelona, 1982
Time period: 1900–1970s
Setting: Unnamed South American country based on Chile

Themes and Issues. Allende's breakthough novel is the story of several generations of the Trueba family and the connections between politics, family, and the supernatural. The work, which tells the story of a powerful family through a female perspective, presents women as strong and powerful, in contrast with the Latin American tradition of male dominance. All of the female characters are faced with brutality and subjugation in one form or another but are able to overcome their tormentors. In the novel women represent morality, while the men symbolize authoritarianism, violence, and repression. For several of the female characters, magic is one means by which they overcome oppression. A final theme of the work is that people cannot escape the consequences of their actions and that choices made at one point can come back to haunt a person later in life.

The Plot. *The House of the Spirits* begins near the turn of the twentieth century in a Latin American nation that is based on Chile. There are three central female characters. The first is Clara de Valle, who is clairvoyant. After her sister Rosa dies, Clara marries Rosa's fiancé, Estaban Trueba. Trueba, one of three main male characters, turns out to be a demanding figure; he is a staunch conservative and becomes a powerful politician. The second main female character, Blanca, the daughter of Estaban and Clara, refuses to stay in an arranged marriage. Meanwhile Estaban Trueba rapes one of his workers, who then has an illegitimate child. Trueba's illegitimate son gives him a grandson, Estaban García, who is enraged because, although he is related to Estaban Trueba, his illegitimate status will prevent him from sharing the power and wealth of the Trueba family. Estaban García becomes a member of the nation's military, helps to overthrow the democratically elected government, and brutally tortures people. The third female character is Alba, the granddaughter of Estaban and Clara, and it is she who narrates the story. She becomes a victim of torture because of her love affair with Miguel, who is a revolutionary fighting against the conservatives and the military in the nation.

LONG FICTION

1982   The House of the Spirits
1984   Of Love and Shadows
1987   Eva Luna
1991   The Infinite Plan
1994   Paula
1999   Daughter of Fortune
2000   Portrait in Sepia
2001   The City of Beasts

SHORT FICTION AND COLLECTIONS

1988   The Stories of Eva Luna
1990   "An Act of Vengeance"
1997   Aphrodite

PLAYS

1971   El embajador
1973   La balada del Medio Pelo
1974   Los siete espejos

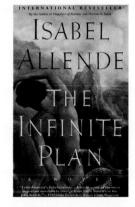

As in René Magritte's *Posies Already Prepared,* a world dominated by the rigid lines of male authority hems in but doesn't overwhelm the strength and spirituality of women in *The House of the Spirits.* Allende says the women in the book "are feminists in their fashion; that is, they ask to be free and complete human beings. . . . Each one battles according to her own characteristics and within the parameters of the epoch in which she happens to be living."

The book follows the rise and fall of Estaban's power. Even as he gains political and economic power, Clara resists his dominance by going into monthlong trances and generally living in the spirit world. Blanca also evades his control and has an affair with a man from the lower class. Estaban García resents his exclusion from the Trueba clan and joins the military as a means to gain power and retaliate against his grandfather. As her mother had done, Alba also becomes involved with a man, Miguel, who is socially unacceptable to Estaban Trueba. In the book's climax Alba is tortured by her cousin in an effort at revenge against his grandfather. The military takeover seals the fate of Estaban Trueba by transferring political power from his class to the military generals. At the end of the novel, his wife has died, his daughter has gone into exile, and his power is gone. However, his granddaughter has survived torture and ultimately triumphs by not giving in to the regime.

Analysis. *The House of the Spirits* is notable for a variety of reasons. First, the work is a feminist critique of the male-dominated society of Latin America at the time, and it describes the strength and inner power of women, even when facing great difficulties. Second, the book is important for its criticism of the brutality and repression of the military regime in Chile. Third and finally, the novel is an important example of the use of magic realism to portray both history and the complexities of the family.

SOURCES FOR FURTHER STUDY

Agosin, Marjorie, and Celeste Kostopulos-Cooperman. *Tapestries of Hope, Threads of Love: The Arpillera Movement in Chile, 1974–1994.* Santa Fe: University of New Mexico Press, 1996.

Hart, Patricia. *Narrative Magic in the Fiction of Isabel Allende.* Rutherford, NJ: Fairleigh Dickinson University Press, 1989.

Rojas, Sonia Riquelme, and Edna Aguirre Rehbein, eds. *Critical Approaches to Isabel Allende's Novels.* New York: P. Lang, 1991.

PAULA
Genre: Novel
Subgenre: Memoir
Published: New York, 1994
Time period: Late 1900s.
Setting: Latin America and the United States

Themes and Issues. Following the death of her daughter, Paula, Allende attempted to work through the emotional loss by writing about her own life and the importance to her of her daughter. The central themes of the book revolve around the emotional joy of the experiences Allende shared with her daughter and the deep sense of loss that came with Paula's death. *Paula* evokes the emptiness felt by a parent who outlives her child. The work is mainly a retelling of Allende's life, but the author has added and changed some aspects so that it is not truly a nonfiction work (in fact, in the Spanish version of the title, "a novel" is the subtitle). The author often interjects pure fantasy into the story and describes her thoughts and imaginings, as well as the actual events of her life. Ultimately, *Paula* is really two stories. The first is the life of Allende, and the second is the life of her daughter. By the end of the work, however, the reader has learned more about Allende than about Paula.

The Plot. *Paula* is the life story of Allende with special attention focused on the birth, life, and death of her daughter. Allende begins with descriptions of her youth in Chile, with special attention to her relationship with her grandparents. She also describes her memories of her uncle Salvador Allende, who was later assassinated during the military coup in 1973. The work provides considerable insight into the influences that shaped Allende's view of the world. She meticulously describes her relationships with her own mother and grandmother and her distant, if not nonexistent, relationships with her father and stepfather. Allende also describes her experiences as a journalist and the difficulties she faced when she first endeavored to publish *The House of the Spirits*.

Allende's children (top), Nicolás and Paula, in 1969. He was three and she was six. Paula grown up in 1991 (inset), the year before she died. Porphyria, inherited from her father, caused her to drop into a coma. She spent the last six months of her life at Allende's home in California. Just as *The House of the Spirits* began as a letter to Allende's dying grandfather, *Paula* started as the letter that Allende wrote to her daughter at her bedside. "My soul is choking in sand," Allende wrote. "I cannot string together two thoughts, much less immerse myself in creating a new book. I plunge into these pages in an irrational attempt to overcome my terror."

In *Paula*, Allende describes how the book began as a letter to Paula while she lay dying with porphyria at the age of 28. Allende begins by addressing her daughter: "Listen Paula. I am going to tell you a story, so that when you wake up you will not feel so lost." Allende began writing in an effort to find a reason to go on living after Paula's death. She details her emotional struggles as her daughter lay in a coma. She felt as if she alone was fighting to keep death away from Paula: "Death wanders freely through the hallways, and my task is to distract it, so it cannot find your door."

The book can be divided into two broad parts. The first section deals with Allende's early life and the onset of Paula's porphyria. The second section describes how Allende

Isabel Allende was influenced primarily by the events and people in her life. The stories she was told as a youth by her grandparents encouraged her imagination and provided background for her later work. From her grandmother she acquired a fascination with magic and the supernatural. From her grandfather she gained a love of reading and storytelling.

Perhaps most significant, the tragedy and turmoil she experienced during her life motivated her to write. Allende has frequently asserted that had she never gone into exile, she would have remained a Chilean journalist and would never have written long fiction. As it was, she did not write her first novel until she was 40 years old. The political repression of her family reinforced her feminist outlook and was the inspiration for works such as *The House of the Spirits* and *Of Love and Shadows.* The concurrent personal tragedies she faced also contributed to her work. The death of her daughter, Paula, for instance, moved her to write the memoir *Paula.*

Allende was also influenced by existing trends in Latin American literature, including the magic realism of the Colombian author Gabriel García Márquez, who won the 1982 Nobel Prize for his work. She grew up reading the works of other Latin American authors who deftly combined the realities of political repression and the overarching importance of family with a strong belief in magic and the supernatural.

General Augusto Pinochet rides to his inauguration as Chile's president. He overthrew Salvador Allende in 1973 and arrested 130,000 people during the three years that followed. Even after allowing himself to be removed in a referendum—he stepped down in 1990—he kept command of the armed forces. Remembering the coup, Allende would say: "A couple of generations of Chileans have lived in limbo, not knowing exactly what happened that Tuesday, September 11, 1973, not knowing who Salvador Allende was or what their country was like before the dictatorship. The collective memory had been brutally smothered. Chile needs to dig up its past in order to heal and mature."

brought her daughter back to California to die once all hope of recovery had passed.

Analysis. Although the core of *Paula* deals with death and deep tragedy, the book is not a sad one. Instead, Allende chooses to concentrate on happy memories of her life and her daughter. The book has numerous humorous anecdotes and touching stories of both mother and daughter. In it Allende continues to use the supernatural and magic to weave her stories. For instance, Allende realizes that she must go on with her life after Paula appears in a vision and comforts her. However, the most significant aspect of *Paula* is the insight that it gives readers into the events and people that influenced Allende's writings.

SOURCES FOR FURTHER STUDY

Cole, Melanie, Valerie Menard, Barbara Tidman, and Mitchell Lane. *Famous People of Latin Heritage.* Vol. 9. New York: Mitchell Lane, 1997.

Fister, Barbara. *Third World Women's Literature: A Dictionary and Guide to Materials in English.* Westport, CT.: Greenwood Press, 1995.

Rodden, John, and Virginia Invernizzi. *Conversations with Isabel Allende.* Houston: University of Texas, 1999.

DAUGHTER OF FORTUNE

Genre: Novel
Subgenre: Historical magic realism
Published: New York, 1999
Time period: 1840s
Setting: Chile and California

Themes and Issues. Unlike many of her other novels, *Daughter of Fortune* is a historical work, set mainly in California during the gold rush of 1849. On one level the novel is about the life journey of a woman who must overcome enormous obstacles to find happiness. As such the work continues the feminist themes of Allende's earlier works by having the female protagonist initially sacrifice all for love. She finds true love only after she has achieved freedom and independence from the constraints of her culture by establishing a new identity in the United States. On another level the book explores the issues of class and race as they affected both Chile and the United States in the nineteenth century. The characters in the book come from different economic backgrounds and different ethnic backgrounds. In addition, the main character, Eliza Sommers, spends years disguised as a man. This device allows Allende to also explore issues of how gender relates to the identity that society ascribes to an individual, as well as the identity derived from one's personality.

The Plot. *Daughter of Fortune* is the story of the life of Eliza, who is Chilean but is raised by a British sister and brother, Rose and Jeremy Sommers, after she is orphaned as a young girl. Rose and Jeremy raise Eliza in a very strict fashion. They want her to grow up to be a proper young English lady. The contempt the Sommerses have for Latin Americans and Catholicism is demonstrated when Rose states that Eliza was "sent by God to be brought up in the solid principles of the Protestant faith and the English language." Eliza becomes the daughter that Rose never had and represents all of the hopes and aspirations of the older woman. The main goal of her adoptive parents is to arrange a proper and fitting marriage for their daughter.

Eliza, however, falls in love with a Chilean clerk, Joaquín, who works for Jeremy. Despite opposition from Rose and Jeremy because of the class differences, Eliza seeks to marry Joaquín anyway; she becomes pregnant before they are married. Meanwhile, Joaquín leaves Chile to seek his fortune in San Francisco during the gold rush of 1849. Although she is pregnant, Eliza sets out to find her lover in California. On the way, Eliza has a miscarriage and is treated by a Chinese doctor, Tao Chi'en. The two become friends and ultimately realize that they are soul mates.

Still, Eliza seeks to marry Joaquín, who has become an outlaw. In an effort to find him, she disguises herself as a man and scours the countryside. As she learns more about Joaquín, Eliza realizes that her love for him has faded. Ultimately, Joaquín is murdered, and his death allows Eliza to express her true love for Tao Chi'en, who in the meantime, in shedding his traditional Chinese identity and becoming more modern and American in nature, has undergone his own transformation.

Analysis. Writing in her usual style, Allende incorporates elements of magic and mysticism in the novel. Eliza has a mystical quality that she shares with many of the female characters in Allende's other works. In addition, Allende devotes enormous detail to each of the major characters so that the reader understands their influences and motivations. The author even includes a lengthy passage in the book describing Tao Chi'en's experiences in China before he left for the United States. Noteworthy above all is that the dominant characters in the work are women, including Eliza, the protagonist; Rose Sommers; and the family maid, Mama Fresia.

SOURCES FOR FURTHER STUDY

Fister, Barbara. *Third World Women's Literature: A Dictionary and Guide to Materials in English.* Westport, CT: Greenwood Press, 1995.

Hart, Patricia. *Narrative Magic in the Fiction of Isabel Allende.* Rutherford, NJ: Fairleigh Dickinson University Press, 1989.

Rodden, John, and Virginia Invernizzi. *Conversations with Isabel Allende.* Houston: University of Texas Press, 1999.

Rojas, Sonia Riquelme, and Edna Aguirre Rehbein, eds. *Critical Approaches to Isabel Allende's Novels.* New York: P. Lang, 1991.

Other Works

OF LOVE AND SHADOWS (1984). In her second novel, *Of Love and Shadows,* Allende continues the themes she developed in *The House of the Spirits.* This book also takes place in a Latin American nation that is controlled by a military dictatorship. The central character in the work is a girl, Irene Beltran, who comes from a wealthy family. Irene is engaged to Gustavo Morante, an army captain who oversees political torture and repression. However, she falls in love with someone from a lower social class—a photographer, Francisco Leal. Together the two undertake an investigation into the disappearance of a young girl with mysterious powers. Their effort leads to discoveries of widespread government-sponsored torture and execution.

In the book Irene and Francisco must make a choice between family loyalty and love. In addition, they must decide whether or not to risk their own lives and love in order to learn the truth about the military regime and expose its repression. The pair chooses to do what is right, even though there are costs to family and themselves. Along the way their investigation leads them into encounters with the supernatural, and as in all of her other novels, Allende incorporates a number of magical episodes and characters. The author also spends considerable time describing the scenery and setting of the story.

PORTRAIT IN SEPIA (2000). In *Portrait in Sepia,* Allende returns to the story and themes that formed the novel *Daughter of Fortune.* Like the earlier novel, *Portrait in Sepia* is set in both San Francisco and Chile. The story is also linked to Eliza Sommers and Tao Chi'en, the protagonists of the earlier work. The novel is a tale of reminiscence in which the main character, Auora del Valle, reviews her life in an effort to remember her early childhood, which she has blocked out. The title comes from the lines that end the novel: "The tone for telling my life is closer to that of a portrait in sepia" (a murky or brownish color associated with very old photographs).

At age 30 Aurora is unhappy with her life. She has been forced into an unhappy marriage and is plagued by nightmares that she thinks

Agustín Llona Cuevas (left), Allende's grandfather and head of the household where she did much of her growing up. She remembered his "proud bearing, the calm dignity of the self-made man who has marched straight down the road of life and expects nothing more." Her "Tata" thought comfort sapped the health, and he liked to answer "direct questions with a different question, so that even though I knew his character to the core, I know very little about his ideology." Allende's grandmother (right), Isabel Barros Moreira, when young. Allende recalls in the semi-fictional *Paula*: "I grew up listening to stories about my grandmother's ability to foretell the future, read minds, converse with animals, and move objects with her gaze. Everyone says that once she moved a billiard table across the room, but the only thing I ever saw move in her presence was an insignificant sugar bowl that used to skitter erratically across the table at tea time." The spirits warned "Memé" that Allende's mother and father would have a disastrous marriage.

are linked to events that occurred during her childhood. However, she cannot remember anything that happened before age five. Hence, to a large degree the story is about memory and its power over an individual's personality. During the retelling of her life, she discovers the links that tie together three generations of her family with Eliza and Tao Chi'en, two of the protagonists from *Daughter of Fortune*.

Aurora is the daughter of a wealthy Chilean and a half-Chinese mother. Her father refuses to accept responsibility for Aurora, and her mother dies in childbirth. Aurora is raised initially by her maternal grandparents and then by her paternal grandparents. As in earlier works, in this novel the central character's grandmother, Paulina del Valle, plays an im-

portant role in the story and is responsible for the move that brings Aurora to Chile. Aurora's fascination with memory leads her to become a photographer, and her work captures the history of Chile at the turn of the century. Aurora ultimately solves her mystery, and this resolution serves as the key to her future happiness.

THE INFINITE PLAN (1991). *The Infinite Plan* marked a number of firsts for Allende. It was her first novel set entirely in the United States and her first novel in which the central character is a man. The book is based loosely on the life of her husband, William Gordon. Although she writes about issues of discrimination and inequality in the United States, there is no military dictatorship, and the degree of oppression faced by many of the characters does not compare with that found in her earlier novels. The novel is set in the 1940s and follows the life of Gregory Reeves, whose family eventually settles in a Hispanic area of Los Angeles after the father falls ill while on a preaching tour that emphasizes God's "infinite plan."

The story examines the culture clash that Reeves faces as he grows up in a society that has Spanish as the primary language and has a culture and traditions different from those he is used to. A Hispanic couple, Pedro and Immaculada Morales, becomes the young man's surrogate family. The Morales family offers Reeves the closeness and intimacy that his own family is unable to supply. Reeves meets a number of intriguing characters during the unfolding of the story, including Cyrus, an aging communist who promotes ideas of social justice. The inclusion of Cyrus gives Allende the opportunity to write about the inequalities in the United States and the need for people to help the disadvantaged. Reeves faces a variety of dangers, at first from gangs in Los Angeles and then during the Vietnam War, but he survives to become a successful lawyer in San Francisco. However, his professional success is clouded by problems in his personal life, including alcohol abuse and family neglect. Ultimately, he finds true love by returning to his roots and ends up with an unnamed Hispanic woman (who, as it happens, narrates the story).

Resources

Since Isabel Allende writes only in Spanish, there are few major resource collections in English. Nonetheless, there are a number of institutions and organizations of interest to students of Allende.

Bedford/St. Martin's Press. This publishing firm maintains a Web site that contains links to other sites about Allende and specific works of hers (www. bedfordstmartins.com/litlinks/fiction/allende.htm).

Isabel Allende Web Site. This site was developed and is maintained by the author herself. It contains interviews, lectures, and summaries of her major works. The site also provides a time line of Allende's life and answers to frequently asked questions about the author (www.isabelallende.com).

Las Mujeres. A Web site that celebrates Latin American female writers. The site contains an unpublished essay by Allende that she used to end a period of writer's block. The site also provides reviews of Allende's works that have been adapted for stage and screen (www.lasmujeres.com/Allende.htm).

Postcolonial Studies at Emory University. This organization, at Emory University in Atlanta, Georgia, promotes the work of authors from around the world, including Latin America. The university's English department maintains a Web page that has a brief biography of Allende and an overview of her works, as well as links to other sites of interest (www.emory.edu/ENGLISH/Bahri/Allende.html).

TOM M. LANSFORD

W. H. Auden

BORN: February 21, 1907, York, England
DIED: September 28/29, 1973, Vienna, Austria
IDENTIFICATION: Midcentury English poet (an American citizen from 1946), as well as a dramatist, librettist, translator, and critic.

SIGNIFICANCE: W. H. Auden was a master of verse forms and styles. His work progressed from lyrics of isolation in the late 1920s and early 1930s through socially conscious poems in the later 1930s into Christian and other moral poetry in the 1940s, with light verse and love poetry throughout. Some critics believe Auden's early work is his most important, but others, perhaps most, find major poetry at all phases of his career. He also wrote or collaborated on plays (mainly in the 1930s) and opera libretti (mainly in the 1950s and 1960s). He published four books of criticism, with many reviews and other incidental writings left uncollected at his death. Auden is widely regarded as the major poet of his generation.

Wystan Hugh Auden was born on February 21, 1907, in York, England. His father was a medical doctor with interests in psychology and archaeology. His university-educated mother was a devout Christian (after her death Auden dedicated his most explicitly Christian work, *For the Time Being,* to her memory). He had two older brothers.

Childhood. Before Auden was two, his father became the school medical officer for Birmingham, England. Auden's youthful imagination was influenced by images of factory furnaces and warehouses, of lead mines and rusting equipment, and of limestone landscapes—the lead mines and limestone having been encountered during his school days. His mother took him as a child to the more elaborate services in the Church of England; she also encouraged him to play the piano and sing

Wystan Hugh Auden in 1928, the year he took a degree at Oxford and published his first book, the slim and privately printed *Poems.* His Oxford tutor claimed to remember this exchange from when Auden was a new student: "And what are you going to do, Mr. Auden, when you leave the university?" "I am going to be a poet." "Well, in that case you should find it very useful to have read English." "You don't understand, I'm going to be a great poet."

Early Schooling. Like most other English children of his class, Auden was sent away to public schools (similar to private schools in America). He met Christopher Isherwood, a lifelong friend, during this period. Auden expected to become a mining engineer; but he eventually realized that lead mines were images of psychological importance to him, not a profession. He began writing poetry in 1922, when he was in the English equivalent of high school.

Oxford. Auden attended Christ Church, one of the colleges at Oxford University, in the fall of 1925. He did poorly on his final examinations at the end of his three years, but in Anglo-Saxon and William Langland's Middle English poetry, he found influential models for some of his later works. At Oxford he made friends with others who, along with Christopher Isherwood, would one day be included as members of the so-called Auden generation—Cecil Day-Lewis, Louis MacNeice, and Stephen Spender.

By this time Auden knew he was homosexual in basic orientation. Nonetheless, despite his continuing sexual activity, Auden harbored guilt feelings or convictions of sinfulness about his homosexuality to some degree throughout his adulthood. (The two biographies listed below give many details of Auden's sexual life, as well as of his long relationship with Chester Kallman, which began in April 1939 and lasted the rest of Auden's life, though it was evidently sexual in nature only until July 1941.)

Germany. After Oxford, Auden spent 10 months in Germany, from October 1928 through July 1929. Reacting to this post–World War I period with its Great Depression, Auden perceived people's personal problems as being psychosomatic (an interpretation based on Freud and other psychologists). Somewhat later, he viewed social problems in rather more general Marxist terms.

England and Journeys. After his trip to Germany, Auden worked as a tutor and as a schoolteacher for several years, publishing his first standard book of poems in 1930. His most Marxist poem, "A Communist to Others," appeared in a journal in 1932; when it was added to a collection in 1936, Auden changed the first word from "Comrades" to "Brothers" and removed the title from the poem. It was later dropped from his collections. A defining moment for Auden occurred in June 1933, in the orchard of a school in which he was teaching: Auden and three others were talking when Auden suddenly felt overcome by what he later called a "vision of agape"—a love of one's neighbors as oneself. (At least one of his companions felt the same thing.)

Auden had a brief association with the New York–based Group Theatre, which staged his play *The Dance of Death* in 1934 and later three plays written in collaboration with Isherwood. In 1936 Louis MacNeice and Auden visited

The novelist Christopher Isherwood, left, sets off with Auden in 1938 to write about China and its struggle to hold off Japan. "We'll have a war all of our very own," said Auden, who had been one of a number of writers to visit Spain and witness the fight there against fascist insurgents. Soon after publication of their book, *Journey to a War*, the friends abandoned Europe and revolution for the United States. Auden and Isherwood had met as boys; finding each other again as young men, they started a friendship that lasted for decades. The young Auden would scrap words and lines of his poetry to meet Isherwood's standards.

Iceland and published *Letters from Iceland* the next year. From January through March 1937 Auden was in Spain during that country's civil war. The closing of churches greatly bothered him although at the time he had abandoned his Christian beliefs. Later that year, Auden met Charles Williams, who worked for the Oxford University Press; Auden said that, although he met Williams only twice, "For the first time in my life, [I] felt myself in the presence of personal sanctity." In 1940 he was much influenced by Williams's *The Descent of the Dove*, a

HIGHLIGHTS IN AUDEN'S LIFE

1907	Wystan Hugh Auden is born on February 21 in York, England.
1908	Auden family moves to the area of Birmingham, England.
1915–1920	Auden meets Christopher Isherwood at Saint Edmund's Preparatory School.
1920–1925	Boards at Gresham's School, Holt, Norfolk.
1925–1928	Is a scholarship student at Christ Church, Oxford; at Oxford meets Cecil Day-Lewis, Louis MacNeice, and Stephen Spender.
1928	Stephen Spender publishes a pamphlet of Auden's poems.
1928–1929	Auden lives in Germany.
1930	*Poems* is published.
1933	Auden experiences the "vision of agape."
1934–1938	Is associated with the Group Theatre, which presents four of his plays (three in collaboration with Isherwood).
1936	Visits Iceland with MacNeice.
1937	Publishes *Letters from Iceland,* a joint work with MacNeice; goes to Spain during the Spanish Civil War; meets Charles Williams.
1938	Visits China with Isherwood during the Sino-Japanese War.
1939	*Journey to a War,* a joint work with Isherwood, is published; Auden moves to the United States and settles in the New York area; meets Chester Kallman.
1940	Returns to Christian belief.
1946	Becomes an American citizen.
1949	Gives the Page-Barbour Lectures at the University of Virginia (they are published as *The Enchafèd Flood* the next year).
1956–1961	Serves as professor of poetry at Oxford University (his lectures were the basis of 14 of the 34 essays and notes published in *The Dyer's Hand* in 1962).
1958	Buys a house in Austria and lives there springs and summers.
1967	Gives the first T. S. Eliot Memorial Lectures at the University of Kent (published as *Secondary Worlds* the next year).
1973	Dies in Vienna, Austria.

Two Great Plays by
W. H. AUDEN
CHRISTOPHER ISHERWOOD

The Dog Beneath the Skin
The Ascent of F6

Auden in his sixties, posing. In the years just before his death, he returned to the college of Christ Church at Oxford. To some of the students he was a relic, to others a sort of human monument. One said, "He could have stood on his head in the quad talking Serbo-Croat and we'd still have thought him great." Auden became friends with a local church dignitary, who would remember him as "a husk of a great man . . . battered, rather tired, more sick, I suppose, than anyone knew."

War, and they produced *Journey to a War* the next year. While in New York on their way back from China, Auden and Isherwood decided to move to America, and they did so in 1939.

New York. One of Auden's original reasons for moving to New York seems to have been to escape what he considered a political role in Britain. His experience of the divisions in the republican side during the Spanish Civil War left him dubious about political action; he also no longer believed that poetry changed society. Reaching New York on January 26, 1939, Auden also hoped to be able to make a living more easily.

Auden began searching for a moral basis for life, not least because he no longer assumed mankind was naturally good. By October 1940 he had begun attending church again and reading theology, soon including the works of Paul Tillich and Reinhold Niebuhr. His Christian search and then regained faith led him to write four long poems between 1939 and 1947. The title of the last of these, *The Age of Anxiety,* was sometimes used as a term for the period.

history of the Christian Church. Williams had been instrumental in getting the Danish philosopher Søren Kierkegaard's theological works published in English; Auden, probably inspired by a passage in *The Descent of the Dove,* read them. In "A Thanksgiving" (1974), Auden said Kierkegaard, Williams, and C. S. Lewis were basic to his return to Christian faith. One of Auden's epigrams, beginning "If all our acts are conditioned behaviour" (1972), presents an argument parallel to a position advanced in Lewis's *Miracles* (1947). *Miracles* was written too late to influence Auden's return to the Christian faith but the parallelism indicates an intellectual agreement between the two men.

In 1938 Isherwood and Auden went to China, to see something of the Sino-Japanese

Later Years. Auden became a U.S. citizen in 1946. After 1949 there was little essential change in his life. He lived part of each year— spring and summer—in Italy and then later in Austria. In autumns and winters in New York, he earned his living as a man of letters. For example, from 1951 until 1962, he was one of the three judges reviewing books for the Readers' Subscription and then the Mid-Century Book Clubs. His poem "On the Circuit" (1964) describes his poetry-reading tours.

Near the end of his life, in 1972, Auden gave up living in New York during half years and stayed in a cottage on the grounds of Christ Church, Oxford. He died of a heart attack, after giving a poetry reading in Vienna, Austria, during the night of September 28/29, 1973.

The Writer's Work

W. H. Auden is mainly known for his poetry, both short and long; but he also wrote plays, opera libretti, criticism, and translations. The poetry is the focus of this section.

Short Poems. Auden's *Poems* (1930) can be considered modernist lyrics—sometimes obscure in setting, sometimes with pronouns without antecedents, sometimes without subjects for verbs, often with wartime or exile imagery, often dealing with the isolation of the individual or with psychological illness. The poems are sometimes in free verse, sometimes in stanzas. In his second volume, *On This Island* (1937), Auden's command of verse forms becomes clearer, and he includes, for example, a sestina, an imitation ballad, several sonnets, and several song lyrics intended for music. Auden turns his serious focus often onto the group as the cure for isolation and for problems with society. His content is generally clearer.

By 1940, in *Another Time,* Auden had written his most famous love poem, "Lullaby." Auden begins imitating Greek and Roman stanzas in this collection and begins using syllabic verse (verse in which the lines consist of a certain number of syllables, sometimes rhymed, sometimes not). In *About the House* (1965), Auden starts using Japanese forms—tanka and haiku. The above-listed verse forms are fewer than half the types Auden composed in.

One characteristic of Auden's mature style (perhaps learned from William Langland's *Piers Plowman,* which he admired at Oxford) is the use of allegorical personifications of such concepts as history, death, justice, nightmare. For the most part, Auden's serious poetry is idea oriented. His vocabulary is broad, both colloquial and learned (he owned and read a copy of the then 13-volume *Oxford English Dictionary*); his interests included science, politics, psychiatry, and theology.

Long Poems. Traditionally, a great poet is expected to have an important long, unified poem to his credit. Whether or not this expectation was the reason, Auden wrote several long poems, all in different verse forms. The

The poet looks rumpled but intact in a photograph that captures his clothes and surroundings in one of their more orderly phases. By one account, the reason Auden's face thickened and creased was a medical condition known as Touraine-Solente-Gole syndrome.

earliest effort he retained in later collections is "Letter to Lord Byron," from *Letters from Iceland*. The easiest to read of Auden's long poems, it is an autobiographical, meandering discussion, in rhyme royal stanzas, of the role of the poet in the modern world.

At the time of Auden's move to America and his return to Christian belief, he wrote four long poems. "New Year Letter" (in *The Double Man*) is written in iambic tetrameter couplets: "Art is not life and cannot be / A midwife to society." The influence of Charles Williams's *Descent of the Dove* is strong in the last part of the poem.

The more explicitly Christian works are "For the Time Being: A Christmas Oratorio" and "The Sea and the Mirror: A Commentary on Shakespeare's *The Tempest*" (both in *For the Time Being*). The first poem takes a musical form, the oratorio, and expands the "songs" into longer poems (or, in two cases, prose). The latter contains speeches by the characters in Shakespeare's play after the action of the play is over (one is in prose).

The last of the four is *The Age of Anxiety: A Baroque Eclogue*. Much of it is written in an alliterative meter imitative of the Anglo-Saxon (four stresses each line, with the third stress alliterating with at least one of the first two). The poem's four characters (who meet in a bar) are based on the characteristics of the four personality types described by the psychologist Carl Jung: intuition (Quant), thinking (Malin), feeling (Rosetta), and sensation (Emble). The content is in part based on theological ideas of Reinhold Niebuhr.

Summary. Auden is one of those poets who wrote many poems—both serious and light, in his case. Inevitably, his work is uneven. He is a truthful poet, that is, he often ignores social manners. He is an intellectual poet: some of his poems—not all—are difficult. At his best he is one of the major poets of the twentieth century.

BIBLIOGRAPHY

Bucknell, Katherine, and Nicholas Jenkins, eds. *Auden Studies*. 3 vols. Oxford: Clarendon Press, 1990, 1994, 1995.

Callan, Edward. *Auden: A Carnival of Intellect*. New York: Oxford University Press, 1983.

Carpenter, Humphrey. *W. H. Auden: A Biography*. Boston: Houghton Mifflin, 1981.

Auden proclaimed his views on everything from English martinis to Beethoven's sexual orientation. He warned a friend that he saw himself "as the Mad Clergyman," preaching sense but throwing in a lot of fireworks. "The trouble with most congregations," he said, "is that either they refuse to listen to a word, or else they swallow everything quite literally."

One of the continuing inspirations in W. H. Auden's life and thought was a love of the Teutonic cultures, those of Germany, Iceland, and Anglo-Saxon England. His father, who read German and Danish, thought that Auden was an Icelandic name and read his son the Norse myths. Auden told of hearing J. R. R. Tolkien lecture at Oxford and especially of his reading a passage from *Beowulf* in the original Anglo-Saxon. "I was spell-bound. This poetry, I knew, was going to be my dish."

Indeed it was. After graduation Auden went to Germany in order to learn the language and culture. In his first play, *Paid on Both Sides* (the title being a translation of a phrase from *Beowulf*), one verse passage employs the typically Teutonic accentual four-beat line, and the content of the play was influenced by the Icelandic sagas Auden had read in translation. The last line of the short poem "The Secret Agent" is a translation of the last line of another Anglo-Saxon poem, "Wulf and Eadwacer." Auden's long poem *The Age of Anxiety* uses (predominantly) the alliterative meter.

Auden also kept track of Tolkien's writings; he read *The Hobbit*, the essay "On Fairy-Stories," and with great enthusiasm *The Lord of the Rings*. He wrote both reviews and essays about *The Lord of the Rings* and, if Tolkien had not discouraged him, would have written a short book on the trilogy. After Tolkien and Auden had exchanged letters and met, Tolkien wrote an Anglo-Saxon poem (with a modern English translation), "For W. H. A.," for Auden's 60th birthday, and Auden wrote "A Short Ode to a Philologist," which ends with praise for Tolkien. Auden's "On the Circuit," about poetry readings, mentions enjoying meeting "an addict of Tolkien." Later on, when Auden, in collaboration with Paul B. Taylor, translated *The Elder Edda: A Selection from the Icelandic,* he dedicated the translation to Tolkien (one of the selections is the source of the dwarvish names Tolkien uses in *The Hobbit*).

John Ronald Reuel Tolkien, Merton Professor of English Language and Literature at Oxford University. His scholarship fed the creation of *The Lord of the Rings*, the wildly popular epic fantasy that made him one of the best-known writers of the twentieth century. Auden championed the book from publication on, annoying critics and the professor himself by declaring on air that if anyone disliked the trilogy, "I shall never trust their literary judgment about anything again."

Davenport-Hines, Richard. *Auden.* New York: Pantheon Books, 1996. A biography.

Fuller, John. *W. H. Auden: A Commentary.* Princeton, NJ: Princeton University Press, 1998. A revised and expanded version of *A Reader's Guide to W. H. Auden* (1970).

Hecht, Anthony. *The Hidden Law: The Poetry of W. H. Auden.* Cambridge, MA: Harvard University Press, 1993.

Hynes, Samuel. *The Auden Generation: Literature and Politics in England in the 1930s.* London: Bodley Head, 1976.

Jacobs, Alan. *What Became of Wystan: Change and Continuity in Auden's Poetry.* Fayetteville: University of Arkansas Press, 1998.

Mendelson, Edward. *Early Auden.* New York: Viking Press, 1981.

—. *Later Auden.* New York: Farrar, Straus & Giroux, 1999.

Wright, George T. *W. H. Auden.* Rev. ed. New York: Twayne, 1981.

Reader's Guide to Major Works

W. H. Auden is primarily known for his short poems. In 1966, for his *Collected Shorter Poems 1927–1957,* he arranged the poems in four chronological sections, three of them reflecting public periods in his life, such as his move to New York. Edward Mendelson, when editing the *Collected Poems* after Auden's death, added two further sections, covering the period from 1958 until Auden's death in 1973. One poem has been chosen from each of the first four periods: "The Secret Agent" (1927–1932), "A Summer Night" (1933–1938), "The Unknown Citizen" (1939–1947), and "In Praise of Limestone" (1948–1957).

Although the lack of discussion of many other poems is regrettable, the poems chosen offer a good cross section of Auden's best-known poetry. (The Fuller and both Mendelson books listed above give surveys of all these poems, which are sometimes cited by first line; Callan omits the third. The versions discussed here are Auden's last revisions.)

POETRY

1930 Poems (revised 1933)
1932 The Orators: An English Study
1936 Look Stranger! (American title, On This Island)
1940 Another Time
1941 New Year Letter (American title, The Double Man)
1944 For the Time Being
1947 The Age of Anxiety: A Baroque Eclogue
1951 Nones
1955 The Shield of Achilles
1960 Homage to Clio
1965 About the House
1969 City without Walls and Other Poems
1972 Epistle to a Godson and Other Poems
1972 Thank You, Fog: Last Poems
1976 Collected Poems (edited by Edward Mendelson; revised 1991)
1977 The English Auden: Poems, Essays, and Dramatic Writings, 1927–1939 (edited by Edward Mendelson; early versions of works later revised)
1994 Juvenilia: Poems 1922–1928 (edited by Katherine Bucknell)

PLAYS

1930 Paid on Both Sides: A Charade (journal publication)
1933 The Dance of Death
1935 The Dog beneath the Skin; or, Where Is Francis? (with Christopher Isherwood)
1936 The Ascent of F6 (with Christopher Isherwood)
1938 On the Frontier (with Christopher Isherwood)

OPERA LIBRETTI (BY DATE OF PRODUCTION)

1941 Paul Bunyan
1951 The Rake's Progress (with Chester Kallman)
1956 The Magic Flute (with Chester Kallman) (translation and adaptation)

1961 Elegy for Young Lovers (with Chester Kallman)
1966 The Bassarids (with Chester Kallman)
1972 Love's Labour's Lost (with Chester Kallman)

TRAVEL BOOKS (MIXED VERSE AND PROSE)

1937 Letters from Iceland (with Louis MacNeice)
1939 Journey to a War (with Christopher Isherwood)

CRITICISM AND OTHER NONFICTION

1950 The Enchafèd Flood; or, The Romantic Iconography of the Sea
1962 The Dyer's Hand and Other Essays
1969 Secondary Worlds
1970 A Certain World: A Commonplace Book
1973 Forewords and Afterwords (edited by Edward Mendelson)
1994 The Prolific and the Devourer (edited by Edward Mendelson)

"A SUMMER NIGHT"

Genre: Autobiographical poem
Subgenre: Poem with 12 stanzas of
rime couée
Published: England, 1936
Time period: June 1933
Setting: Downs School orchard, Colwall,
Hertfordshire, England

Background. In the essay "The Protestant Mystics" (1964), which is collected in *Forewords and Afterwords* (1973), Auden describes an experience that he calls the "vision of agape," which is reflected in part in this poem. In the summer of 1933, while Auden was teaching at Downs School, he and some of the students slept out in the orchard (first two stanzas). He was sitting out there talking with three of his colleagues when he had a sudden experience of loving his neighbor as himself (at least one other of the four had the same experience), an experience that came from outside of himself

Unison of Many Hearts is the name of this painting by Gerrit Greve. In "A Summer Night" Auden describes a moment in which he glimpsed agape (loving others as oneself). Viewed against the political troubles of the 1930s, the poem can be seen as reconciling individual love with the collective society to come after revolution: "May these delights we dread to lose, / This privacy need no excuse / But to that strength belong, / As through a child's rash happy cries / The drowned parental voices rise / In unlamenting song."

(third and fourth stanzas). The experience faded over the next few days. He seems not to have known what to think of the experience at the time, but when he gathered his short poems into temporal sections, the fact that he began the second section from this date and with this poem is a mark of its importance.

Content. "A Summer Night" (contained in *Look Stranger!*) describes the "vision of agape" experience with metaphors—"The lion griefs loped from the shade / And on our knees their muzzles laid"—not with analytic or theological terminology (except perhaps "dove-like"). The poem goes on to describe the shining moon (stanzas 5 through 7) in order to provide a transition to the situation elsewhere. A rather vague reference to Poland (stanza 8) suggests political problems, and imagery of a flood and rebuilding ("riveting") afterward (stanzas 9 and 10) suggests a revolution (perhaps communistic) and the establishing of a new society. (At the time Auden was concerned with the significance of groups, including communists, in attempts to overcome individual isolation.) The last two stanzas express the hope that this experience of agape may be part of that new society ("that strength"). Auden cannot see his experience outside of his concern for society at the time. Later he thought changes could take place only in the individual or among friends—but that view is not this poem's.

Verse form. *Rime couée* is a six-line stanza, consisting of two lines of iambic tetrameter (rhyming AA), a line of iambic trimeter (B), two more lines of iambic tetrameter (CC), and another line of iambic trimeter (B). It has been used in such earlier English poems as Christopher Smart's "A Song to David" (1763) and William Wordsworth's "The Wishing Gate" (1829).

"THE SECRET AGENT"

Genre: Short modernist poem
Subgenre: Unrhymed sonnet
Published: England, 1930
Setting: Symbolic

Content. "The Secret Agent" (contained in *Poems*) consists of two quatrains and a sestet, divided by spaces between them. In the first four lines the secret agent worries about control of mountain passes; the suggestion is one of warfare, and the agent is caught in some sort of trap. In the second quatrain the agent has located the site for a dam, but his side (simply referred to as "they") has not built a railroad to the site. In the last six lines he is in a city after some weeks in a desert; while in the desert he seems to have dreamed of water and a companion, which were not there when he woke. The poem ends, "They [no antecedent] would shoot," parting the agent and his absent companion. No doubt it is possible to invent a landscape combining mountain passes, a site for a dam, a desert, and a city, but the probability is that these settings are simply used as appropriate to the tone of the poem, whose burden is that the secret agent is isolated and unsupported.

Analysis. One critic (Fuller) says that this is a poem about love: the secret agent represents a person's emotional urges—the desire for a companion expressed in the sestet, for example. "They," who ignore the agent's communications about the dam and who will eventually shoot him, are the conscious will, which does not recognize these urges. The trap of the first quatrain is the limiting social conventions. Another critic (Callan) believes the secret agent is the conscious ego; his attempt to conquer new territory, without appropriate support, is the ego's attempt to control the id; viewed thus, the sestet shows the death wish wishing to stop Eros (in Freud's use of the term). A third critic (Mendelson) briefly suggests that the separation between the agent and the companion may be that between mind and body. What is striking about this early, symbolic poem is that it can mean different things to different readers, who can find support in the poem for their readings. Auden's later poems are seldom so open to differing interpretation.

Identity becomes a riddle in "The Secret Agent." Is he the ego or the emotions? "Control of the passes was, he saw, the key / To this new district, but who would get it?" J. Natal's artwork *Memento Mori,* like Auden's "The Secret Agent," appears to suggest an identity crisis. Many critics, too, have had their own crisis concerning how to interpret this particular Auden poem.

"THE UNKNOWN CITIZEN"

Genre: Satiric poem
Subgenre: Irregularly rhymed, rather proselike free verse
Published: England, 1940
Setting: United States

Background. Auden wrote "The Unknown Citizen" (contained in *Another Time*) in March 1939 after his January move to New York, and his use of "mates" to mean "workplace friends" shows that the British idiom was still with him. Otherwise the poem is remarkably American. The invented string of letters and numbers for the citizen being discussed—JS/07/M/378—starts with JS, probably for John Smith, in American terms, a common man (the M may stand for "male"). "Fudge Motors Inc." combines Ford and Dodge in its name—with a different vowel, to add to the humor.

The faceless hero of "The Unknown Citizen" lived his life through and for organizations, never causing them a moment's trouble. Bureaucrats reporting on him agree, "That, in the modern sense of an old-fashioned word, he was a saint, / For in everything he did he served the Greater Community." Another faceless figure is portrayed in "Untitled," a painting by artist Emily Eveleth.

Analysis. The title "The Unknown Citizen" suggests the marble Tomb of the Unknown Soldier in Arlington National Cemetery, in Arlington, Virginia. The dedication for the "Marble Monument" to this citizen in the parenthesis below the title shows that he *is* known, but known only by a file number (the equivalent of being known by a social security number). In this dedication, although printed in three lines, if the second and third lines are combined, they form a couplet where "378" rhymes with "by the State." So far the poem has established that the government has raised a monument to a citizen. In the body of the poem, the government bureaucrats ("we") speak about the basis for the choice of this citizen: he was an absolutely typical citizen who did not cause trouble—"He was found by the Bureau of Statistics to be / One against whom there was no official complaint." Obviously, in Auden's use of irony, the bureaucrats' approval of such a citizen suggests their approval of an unimaginative, stereotypical life. The irony is clearest in the climactic lines: "Was he free? Was he happy? The question is absurd: / Had anything been wrong, we should certainly have heard." Although America was founded on the basis of freedom and the pursuit of happiness, Auden notes both the personal conformity of many citizens and governmental approval of it.

IN PRAISE OF LIMESTONE

    Genre: Loco-descriptive poem
    Subgenre: Syllabic version of elegiac
      couplets
    Published: England, 1951
    Time period: During Auden's first visit to
      Italy in May 1948
    Setting: Limestone landscape around
      Florence, Italy

Organization. The loco-descriptive poem usually starts with a description of a place (*loco,* from *locus,* is Latin for "place"). *In Praise of Limestone* (from *Nones*) is made up of four verse paragraphs, and Auden spends his first on the "rounded shapes," belowground "caves," pools of water, and walkable distances that make up this landscape. He is interested in the influence of a limestone area on its inhabitants and introduces one person in the first paragraph and others in the second. He sees the men (he does not mention women) as being satisfied with the surface level of things, as being flexible in their attitudes (as limestone is easily shaped by water), not rigidly moral, for example. In the third paragraph he says that those men who are not satisfied with these attitudes—the saints and the militarists—leave for "immoderate soils"; the reckless leave for the sea.

The fourth verse paragraph, in which Auden reaches his conclusions, has caused critical confusion. Auden suddenly addresses a person as "my dear." One critic thinks he is speaking to his dead mother, another that the poem becomes a love poem and he is addressing a beloved. However, two earlier English loco-descriptive poems indicate that this organization is typical. William Wordsworth, in "Lines Composed a Few Miles above Tintern Abbey" (1798), in the last verse paragraph speaks to his sister, "thou my dearest Friend," and Matthew Arnold, in "Dover Beach" (1867), in the last stanza addresses his "love" (assumed to be his wife, for he wrote the poem about the time of his marriage in 1851). Whomever Auden is addressing, the device gives him someone to talk to in the last paragraph.

Analysis. The fourth verse paragraph states that this landscape (along with the people it produces) does have its "worldly duty": to rebuke the rigid personalities of the rest of the world—not just the rigid but those who do not like repetition and who cover up their faults. He gives three examples of the rigid, and then he makes a religious point: no doubt rigid habits are useful if all one has is this world, but if there is forgiveness and a resurrection, then, since "[t]he blessed will not care what angle they are regarded from" (that is, they do not hide aspects of themselves), the openness of those people produced by limestone areas is a valuable example of what salvation will be like for others.

The "best and worst" of humanity are lured away from the surface level of things by other visions, according to Auden's "In Praise of Limestone." Trapped in his tiny box, propelling himself through oblivion, the figure in Michael Bergt's 1997 artwork "The Rower" could be listening to the voice described here: "But the really reckless were fetched / By an older, colder voice, the oceanic whisper: / 'I am the solitude that asks and promises nothing; / That is how I shall set you free. There is no love; / There are only the various envies, all of them sad.'"

Verse form. With his move to America, Auden based some of his poems on the number of syllables per line, after the example of the American poet Marianne Moore. "In Praise of Limestone" is in unrhymed two-line units, the first line having 13 syllables and the second, 11. To make these numbers work, one must sometimes count as one syllable two adjacent vowels (in the first line, the *e* and *o* in "the one" and the *e* and *i* in "the in-") or two vowels with only an *h* between them (in the second line, "-ly home-"), though Auden does not use the elision with an *m* between vowels of classical prosody (that is, for example, "thyme and" of the fourth line counts as two syllables). These two-line syllabic units are Auden's updated version of the elegiac couplets of Greek and Roman poetry (note that "elegiac," in this sense, has no necessary relationship to what the word means in plain English).

SOURCES FOR FURTHER STUDY

Bozorth, Richard R. *Auden's Games of Knowledge: Poetry and the Meaning of Homosexuality.* New York: Columbia University Press, 2001.

Upward, Edward, et al. "'In Praise of Limestone': A Symposium." In *"In Solitude, for Company": W. H. Auden after 1940: Unpublished Prose and Recent Criticism* (vol. 3 of *Auden Studies*), edited by Katherine Bucknell and Nicholas Jenkins. Oxford: Clarendon Press, 1995.

Other Works

PAUL BUNYAN: AN OPERETTA IN TWO ACTS (produced 1941, published 1976). *Paul Bunyan* is the first of Auden's libretti; it was set to music by Benjamin Britten (1913–1976), a major English composer. At the time Britten and Auden were living in New York, and Britten was encouraged by his publisher to write a work for high school productions—hence their use of an American legend. (The first production was mounted at a university campus.) In a prologue and two acts of two scenes each, the work is episodic, with most of the legend of Paul Bunyan (including invented details, such as his marriage and his daughter) narrated in couplets in interludes between the scenes. Bunyan himself, described as being "as tall as the Empire State" Building, speaks from offstage only. What Auden has done is trace the history of the United States—from the prologue, with trees and geese only, to the modern world at the end of act 2—in terms of the lumber industry. Much of the libretto is lighthearted, as in the first scene of act 1, when Sam Sharpey, hawking soups, and Ben Benny, hawking beans, break into parodies of modern commercials. Britten, who did not finish the revisions after the first production, returned to the operetta after Auden's death to establish the music and text for publication.

THE RAKE'S PROGRESS: A FABLE (produced and published, 1951). When Igor Stravinsky (1882–1971)—probably the major twentieth-century composer—wanted to write an opera on a series of etchings titled *The Rake's Progress* by William Hogarth (1697–1764), Auden was recommended to him as a librettist (Auden later brought in Chester Kallman as collaborator). The setting is eighteenth-century England. The plot follows Tom Rakewell, who is loved by Anne Trulove. When Rakewell wishes for wealth, there suddenly appears a man who calls himself Nick Shadow (he is actually the devil), who offers to act as Rakewell's serving man for a year and a day. With the surprise inheritance that Shadow produces, Rakewell goes astray in London. In the second scene of act 3, set in a graveyard a year later, Shadow is ready to carry Rakewell off to hell but gives him a last chance—if Tom names three cards correctly, he avoids damnation. When he does so (despite a trick), the devil descends into the open grave but as a parting shot curses Rakewell with madness. The act's last scene is set in a madhouse, where Rakewell is visited by Anne. The opera was successful, entered the standard opera repertoire, and has since been many times performed.

Anne Trulove, portrayed by Barbara Hendricks, and Tom Rakewell, portrayed by Greg Fedderly (left), frolic in a televised version of *The Rake's Progress.* Auden told the opera's composer, Igor Stravinsky (right), "the chance of working with you is the greatest honour of my life." One colorful writer, noting the striking contrast between Auden and Stravinsky, wrote, ". . . for the shabby, dandruff-speckled, and slightly peculiar-smelling poet (attributes easily offset by his purity of spirit and intellectual punctiliousness) could not have been more unlike the neat, sartorially perfect, and faintly eau-de-cologned composer. At table, too, while the poet demolished his lamb chops, potatoes, and sprouts, as if eating were a chore to be accomplished as quickly as possible, and gulped Stravinsky's carefully-chosen Chateau Margaux oblivious to its qualities, the composer fussed over his food, and sniffed, sipped and savoured the wine." Stravinsky was taken aback to discover that Chester Kallman, Auden's former lover, was also working on the libretto, but he had only praise on reading what they presented him.

THE MAGIC FLUTE: AN OPERA IN TWO ACTS (produced on television and published in 1956). In 1955 the National Broadcasting Company commissioned a new English text of Mozart's opera *The Magic Flute* (*Die Zauberflöte*) from Auden and Kallman. They had done three other translations of libretti, but only this one involved radical rewriting of the original—they reorganized the sequence of musical passages in the second act and turned the prose dialogue between these sung passages (in Emanuel Schikaneder's original German libretto) into verse. In short, their changes were enough for this to be considered a nearly original work. In the preface to the printed version, Auden and Kallman point out that fairy-story material must be handled carefully, since it is archetypal. One of their examples is the struggle between the high priest Sarastro (reason, daylight) and Queen Astrafiammante (instinct, night), which must end when the marriage of Tamino and Pamina reconciles the two sides (the original libretto signals the defeat of the queen but leaves Sarastro unaffected). In their libretto Auden and Kallman add a speech for Sarastro (act 2, scene 2) in which he prepares for his "mission [being] complete" and his loss of power.

For the publication of this libretto in book form, the authors added a "Proem" (by Auden), summarizing the background; a "Postscript: Astrafiammante to the translators" (by both), in which the queen announces, among other things, that she is their muse; and a "Metalogue" (by Auden), a long speech in the middle of the opera for the singer playing Sarastro, explaining that audiences are used to commercials interrupting plots. This speech, in heroic couplets, celebrates the 200th anniversary of Mozart's birth in the year of publication.

The last three operas by Auden and Kallman were not as successful as *The Rake's Progress* in gaining later productions. They wrote *Elegy for Young Lovers* (about an egotistical poet who will sacrifice those around him in order to create great poetry) and *The Bassarids* (a reworking of Euripides' tragedy *The Bacchae*) with the German composer Hans Werner Henze (b. 1926) and *Love's Labour's Lost* (an adaptation of Shakespeare's play) with Nicolas Nabokov (1903–1978). Nevertheless, the libretti are interesting for readers. Auden wrote, in "The World of Opera" (in *Secondary Worlds*), that "Opera is the last refuge of the High style," and indeed, his libretti show him writing in a different, more extravagant style than any he used in his poetry. Auden was the master of many styles.

Resources

The major library holding of W. H. Auden materials is at the Berg Collection of the New York Public Library. The collection's Web site is not useful, but *W. H. Auden, 1907–1973: An Exhibition from the Berg Collection,* edited by Edward Mendelson (New York Public Library, 1980), lists the holdings. In addition, section J in the bibliography cited below lists the notebooks and individual manuscripts in various collections.

Complete Works. As of 2002, the complete edition of Auden's work was itself still a work in progress. All four finished volumes, published by Princeton University Press, have been edited by Edward Mendelson: *Plays and Other Dramatic Writings, 1928–1938,* including works with Christopher Isherwood (1989); *Libretti and Other Dramatic Writings, 1939–1973,* including works with Chester Kallman (1993); *Prose and Travel Books in Prose and Verse, 1926–1938* (1996); and *Prose, 1939–1948* (2002).

W. H. Auden: A Bibliography. Ordinarily, one would check a bibliography only for what an author published, but B. C. Bloomfield and Edward Mendelson's *W. H. Auden: A Bibliography, 1924–1969,* 2nd ed. (Charlottesville: University Press of Virginia, 1972), has more. It lists Auden's appearances on radio and television, with some information as to later publication of some of the talks (section M), released recordings of Auden reading his poems (section N), and musical settings of Auden's verse (section S). In the first appendix it lists all the important criticism of Auden's writings through 1969.

W. H. Auden Society. The best starting place of a Web search for materials on Auden is with the society that bears his name (www.audensociety.org). The site gives a useful secondary bibliography on Auden, and it provides links to other valuable Web pages. It also contains a list of available recordings of Auden reading his poems and another of recordings of the operas for which Auden wrote the libretto.

JOE R. CHRISTOPHER

Mariama Bâ

BORN: 1929, Dakar, Senegal
DIED: 1981, Senegal
IDENTIFICATION: Senegalese novelist known for her exploration of the lives of Muslim women and for her examination of polygamy and the caste system in Africa.

SIGNIFICANCE: Mariama Bâ emerged as a significant writer with the 1979 novel *So Long a Letter,* which brought her critical acclaim and the Noma Award for African writing in 1980. The novel, which is emblematic of all her work, examines the culture shock experienced by two Senegalese women who marry men who claim to embody a modern concept of love but later embrace the Islamic tradition of taking a second wife. Bâ's interest as a writer in conflicting value systems reflects the tensions present in the newly independent Senegal of the 1970s, a country where vast social and cultural changes were in progress while at the same time a resurgence in Islamic fundamentalism was taking place.

The Writer's Life

Childhood. Mariama Bâ is considered to be one of Senegal's most notable francophone novelists. Bâ was born in Dakar, Senegal, in 1929. Her mother died when she was very young, and Bâ was raised by her maternal grandparents in a traditional Muslim environment. Her father was an intellectual who became the first Senegalese minister of health in 1956. He insisted that his daughter have a French secondary education, even though this decision was against the wishes of her grandparents, and as a result Bâ went to the École Normale (Teacher's College) for girls in Rufisque, a city near Dakar, where she attained the highest exam score in 1943 for all of colonial French West Africa. She also published two pieces of writing during her secondary schooling, one of which focused on colonial education.

Marriage and Teaching Career. After obtaining her teaching certificate in 1947, Bâ worked first as an elementary school teacher at the School of Medicine in Dakar for 12 years and then, for health reasons, as a teaching inspector. Early on in her teaching career, she married Obeye Diop, a member of parliament, and had nine children with him. Bâ took a hiatus from writing during the years of her marriage, for she was busy raising nine children, promoting education, and initiating a women's movement in Senegal. Bâ's marriage ended in divorce, an experience that provided inspiration for her first book, *So Long a Letter*. In an interview that followed the publication of the novel, Bâ claimed that *So Long a Letter* was not meant to be read as autobiography. All the same, there are numerous parallels between the life of the

The bustling city of Dakar, the capital of Senegal, first informed Mariama Bâ's conceptions of the world in which she lived. Her accomplishments have left an indelible mark on her homeland. Currently there is a school named after the novelist on nearby Goree Island, a 45-acre island off the coast of Senegal, less than 2 miles from Dakar.

writer and the life of the protagonist: they were roughly the same age at the time of the novel's publication, they were both elementary teachers, they both raised many children, and they both experienced an unsuccessful marriage.

A Writer of Significant Acclaim. *So Long a Letter* is regarded as an important addition to the canon of African literature, since it was one of the first works in sub-Saharan Africa to explore the struggles of Muslim women in Africa, especially those experiences related to the practice of polygamy. It was published as *Une si longue lettre* in 1979 by Nouvelles Éditions Africaines, when Bâ was 51. It received instant acclaim and won her the first Noma Award for writing in Africa, a prize initiated in 1980 and given to the best work produced in both French- and English-speaking Africa. The novel was translated by Modupe Bode-Thomas and published in English by Nigeria's New Horn Press in 1981. Within a few years it was also translated into 15 other languages.

Bâ's second novel, *Scarlet Song,* was published posthumously by Nouvelles Éditions Africaines in 1981 as *Un chant écarlate*. It was translated into English by Dorothy Blair and published by Longman Press in 1986. It concentrates on the problems associated with patriarchal indulgences licensed by polygamy. As in *So Long a Letter,* the taking of a second wife destroys the harmony and equality of an existing marriage and forces the first wife to decide how she will respond to the betrayal of trust. *Scarlet Song* differs from Bâ's first novel, however, in that it also features an interracial marriage. As a result the novel depicts a French woman's attempt to adjust to the entirety of the African value system in Senegal and not just the practice of polygamy.

International Reception. Bâ has attracted a considerable amount of international interest since the publication of *So Long a Letter.* French critics place her in a francophone literary tradition, while other Western critics identify her as a representa-

HIGHLIGHTS IN BÂ'S LIFE

1929   Mariama Bâ is born in Dakar, Senegal.

1941   Attends the École Normale (Teacher's College) in Rufisque, a city near Dakar.

1943   Receives highest score in all of West Africa on secondary examination.

1947   Obtains her teaching certificate and works as an elementary teacher for 12 years.

1959   Works as teaching inspector.

1979   *Une si longue lettre* is published in Senegal.

1980   Bâ wins the first Noma Award for writing in Africa.

1981   English version of *So Long a Letter* is published in Nigeria; Bâ dies just before the release of her second novel; *Un chant écarlate* is published posthumously in Senegal.

1986   English version of *Scarlet Song* is published in England.

tive of African women, especially in the context of feminism. African American critics place her work in the body of black women's writing.

Bâ's Activism. Besides writing novels in the later part of her life, Bâ also worked as a journalist of women's issues and participated in several Senegalese women's organizations, including her own association called Soeurs Optimistes Internationales. She has been credited with initiating a feminist movement in Senegal, although she refused to call herself a feminist. She did not agree with the separation of the sexes, and in addition, she was concerned that a feminist agenda could lead to a denigration of the importance of motherhood. Throughout the course of her life, however, in both her writing and her organizing, Bâ promoted the crucial role of women in a developing country, and she concerned herself with issues surrounding polygamy, child custody, and women's legal rights in marriage.

Bâ died in 1981 after a long illness and shortly before the release of *Scarlet Song*. With her early death, Senegal lost one of its most insightful voices on the female condition in Africa.

Men participate in a long-standing cultural tradition, playing koras, stringed gourd instruments, during a festival in Dakar. In her writing, Bâ does not indict men as a group. Instead they are sidestepped, viewed as often too deeply entrenched in their social concepts of gender in order to apprehend the harm their actions create. *So Long a Letter* articulates the pain polygamy triggers in the lives of the women involved. While the cultural practice often serves to divide the multiple wives, in an interview Bâ granted after accepting the inaugural Noma Award for the best African novel of the year, she spoke of the undeniable unity of women, asserting that "there is a cry everywhere, everywhere in the world, a woman's cry is being uttered. The cry may be different but there is still a certain unity."

Issues in Bâ's Fiction. In her writing, Bâ depicts couples who enter into marriages based on equality and mutual respect. The harmonious marriages are destroyed, however, when the husbands are motivated to marry second wives. In offering this tragic perspective on marriage, Bâ demonstrates what befalls women who are caught between diametrically opposed societies, the traditional and the modern. Bâ's novels also celebrate the power of female solidarity that enables women to transcend their suffering. In *So Long a Letter* two friends recover from the collapse of their marriages, largely because of the support they offer each other. In *Scarlet Song* a French woman's abandonment in marriage is exacerbated by her alienation from other women. For Bâ, then, the constancy of friendship is set in contrast with the vulnerability of romantic love. At the same time the compassion that women demonstrate to one another offers a model for what could also be gained within

Motherhood for West African women, such as the Senegalese woman seen here, is a central concern in Bâ's writing, but unlike many other West African women writers, she does not find the role of women as narrowly defined or as claustrophobic. Still her work is not without its radical assertions. Critic Edris Makward has written that Mariama Bâ is "the first African writer to stress unequivocally the strong desire of a new generation of Africans to break away from the age-old marriage customs and adopt a decidedly more modern approach based on free mutual choice and the equality of the two partners."

the context of marriage if spouses remained true to their commitments.

People in Bâ's Fiction. Bâ's characters are very human. They have strong desires for love and friendship and are deeply affected when the bonds they cherish are violated. The male characters in Bâ's works prove incapable of constancy and are easily influenced by the pressures of extended families and their own lustful desires. Bâ's female characters are unique and do not fall into the stereotypical roles often given women in African literature. In *So Long a Letter* Bâ presents a middle-aged woman at the crossroads, dealing with the complex social, moral, and emotional implications that come with her age. In *Scarlet Song* Bâ explores the struggles a French woman must face when adjusting to married life in Senegal, including the disdain of her husband's family.

The Theme of Abandonment. Bâ's writing suggests that all women—regardless of race or class—are vulnerable to abandonment. According

A Senegalese woman poses for this photograph taken in the 1990s. The female characters in Bâ's *So Long a Letter* attempt to, and to an extent succeed in, taking control of their lives. The main protagonist Ramatoulaye ends her letter to her friend Aissatou, which is the basis of the novel, by proclaiming, "I have not given up wanting to refashion my life. Despite everything—disappointments and humiliations—hope still lives within me."

to tradition a man who practices polygamy should follow three principles: treat the wives equally, grant them the same sexual access, and meet all their expenses. Bâ's male characters fall short of these expectations; from this perspective it is the vulgarization of the institution that creates turmoil. On the other hand Bâ can be seen to be criticizing polygamy as a whole for the way that it disfranchises women, especially women in a modern setting where traditional ideas of marriage and caste no longer apply. Whether Bâ is seen to be attacking the institution or the deterioration of its original purposes, it is without question that she prefers monogamous marriages. Before they were disrupted, the marriages in Bâ's novels brought out the complementary nature of men and women and demonstrated the productivity that a well-suited couple could contribute to family, community, and nation.

BIBLIOGRAPHY

Abubakr, Rashidah Ismali. "The Emergence of Mariama Bâ." In *Essays on African Writing: A Re-evaluation,* edited by Abdulrazak Gurnah. Portsmouth, NH: Heinemann, 1993, pp. 24–37.

d'Almeida, Irene Assiba. "The Concept of Choice in Mariama Bâ's Fiction." In *Ngambika: Studies of Women in African Literature,* edited by Carole Boyce Davies and Anne Adams Graves. Trenton, NJ: Africa World Press, 1986, pp. 161–172.

Edson, Laurie. "Mariama Bâ and the Politics of Family." *Studies in Twentieth-Century Literature* 17, no. 1 (winter 1993): 13–25.

Harrell-Bond, Barbara. "Interview with Mariama Bâ." *The African Book Publishing Record* 6 (1980): 209–214.

King, Adele. "The Personal and the Political in the Work of Mariama Bâ." *Studies in Twentieth-Century Literature* 18, no. 2 (summer 1994): 177–188.

Makward, Edris. "Marriage, Tradition and Woman's Pursuit of Happiness in the Novels of Mariama Bâ." In *Ngambika: Studies of Women in African Literature,* edited by Carole Boyce Davies and Anne Adams Graves. Trenton, NJ: Africa World Press, 1986, pp. 271–281.

Nnaemeka, Obioma. "Mariama Bâ: Parallels, Convergence and Interior Space." In *The Growth of African Literature: Twenty-five Years after Dakar and Fourah Bay,* edited by Edris Makward, Thelma Ravell-Pinto, and Aliko Songolo. Trenton, NJ: Africa World Press, 1998, pp. 197–214.

———. "Urban Spaces, Women's Places: Polygamy as Sign in Mariama Bâ's Novels." In *The Politics of (M)othering,* edited by Obioma Nnaemeka. New York: Routledge, 1997, pp. 162–191.

Nwachukwu-Agbada, J. O. J. "'One Wife Be for One Man': Mariama Bâ's Doctrine for Matrimony." *Modern Fiction Studies* 37, no. 3 (autumn 1991): 561–573.

Plant, Deborah G. "Mythic Dimensions in the Novels of Mariama Bâ." *Research in African Literatures* 27, no. 2 (summer 1996): 102–111.

SOME INSPIRATIONS BEHIND BÂ'S WORK

Bâ's writing was greatly affected by her appreciation of the griot musical tradition in Senegal. The griot's role as entertainer is to educate people about societal values and practices through oral literature. Bâ believed that the writer—the contemporary version of the griot—should play a vital role in helping to build a free democratic society. She attempted to do so in her own writing by illustrating the plight of women in a male-dominated society and by suggesting the societal improvements that would occur if women were given the right to full happiness.

Reader's Guide to Major Works

SO LONG A LETTER
Genre: Novel
Subgenre: Epistolary novel
Published: Senegal, 1979
Time period: 1930–1979
Setting: Dakar, Senegal

Themes and Issues. *So Long a Letter* is an epistolary novel containing the extended letter that Ramatoulaye writes to Aissatou during the lengthy seclusion she undergoes, in accordance with Islamic custom, following the death of her husband, Modou. In this letter Ramatoulaye remembers the past she experienced with Aissatou, including their schooling, their marriages, and the betrayals they suffered when their husbands took second wives. The epistolary form allows Ramatoulaye to explore her inner self at the same time that she communicates with Aissatou. The novel, then, is simultaneously a missive to a dearest confidante and a search for self-understanding.

The Plot. Ramatoulaye begins her letter by describing the Islamic funeral traditions, including the requirement that Modou's second wife, Binetou, remain at Ramatoulaye's house during the first days of mourning. Ramatoulaye also describes the *mirasse,* a ritual in which the deceased's most intimate secrets are revealed. Through this ritual she learns that, after abandoning her and their 12 children, Modou showered Binetou with gifts and accumulated massive debt.

Ramatoulaye then remembers her first meeting with Modou at college, where they immediately fell in love. She also recalls the secondary school she and Aissatou attended, the school that prepared them to become "the first pioneers of the promotion of African women." Trained to dismiss tradition, Ramatoulaye ignores her mother's objections and marries Modou. Soon after, Aissatou marries Mawdo, Modou's close friend, even though they are from different castes. After their marriages, the two women work as teachers, raise children, and support the work of their hus-

A West African mosque stretches high above the walled city of Kano in Nigeria. In *So Long a Letter,* Bâ refuses to portray her protagonists as victims of their Islamic beliefs, which in some West African cultures rigidly define the role of women in the family and community. Bâ's strength lies in her gift for drawing complex characters and placing them in multifaceted narratives. For her, religion and cultural tradition are abstract concepts that offer little comfort for those wishing to assign blame for their failures and frustrations. She eschews simplistic or reductive explanations for why Ramatoulaye and Aissatou find themselves in their present situations. Still, as a woman, she is not without her allegiances. Her novel is partially dedicated "To all women and to men of good will," a telling qualification in her citation of her male counterparts.

bands. Faced with difficult in-law situations, they also take comfort in each other.

Meanwhile, Mawdo's mother seeks to undo her son's marriage by finding him a more acceptable second wife and insisting that he marry her. Mawdo agrees, and Aissatou's place is immediately usurped. Consequently, Aissatou leaves Mawdo, taking their four sons and securing employment as an interpreter in the United States. Mawdo is disoriented by her departure, but his grief does not lead him to relinquish the second wife.

Ramatoulaye then narrates her own crisis, which comes three years later, when her husband marries a schoolgirl at the encouragement of the girl's mother. Ramatoulaye learns of the wedding when a group of men visit to inform her it has already taken place. Ramatoulaye's children encourage her to leave, but she decides to stay because of her love for Modou. She prepares to share him according to the precepts of Islamic law, but he spends all his time and money with his new wife, Binetou, instead.

Forty days after Modou's death, his brother informs Ramatoulaye that he will marry her, following the Muslim tradition concerning the fate of a brother's widow. This time Ramatoulaye speaks out, denouncing him and gaining vengeance for the men's earlier visit. Soon after, a former suitor also arrives to propose marriage, but Ramatoulaye rejects him also because she does not love him and she cannot allow herself to become a second wife. Ramatoulaye next writes to Aissatou about her second daughter's illegitimate pregnancy. Ramatoulaye unexpectedly decides to forgive and help this daughter, and she accepts a role that is subordinate to that of the daughter's future husband.

On the last day of her seclusion, Ramatoulaye closes her letter with anticipation over Aissatou's upcoming visit. She also reflects upon her convictions developed in seclusion and concludes that she is open to the idea of women's liberation, though she still believes in the "inevitable and necessary complementarity of man and woman." She hopes that with her new understanding, she will never again have to write "so long a letter."

Analysis. At first glance Ramatoulaye and Aissatou appear to be opposites; one divorces, while the other remains in a polygamous marriage. They are also a study in sameness, however, with their rural upbringing, their progressive education, their controversial romances, and their ultimately unhappy marriages. While Ramatoulaye appears to make the more traditional choice, it eventually wins her the same autonomy. Both emerge from their collapsed marriages better

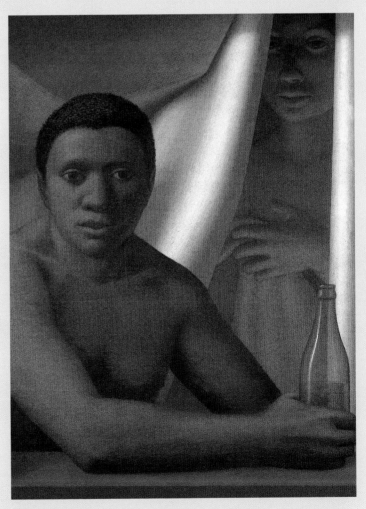

George Tooker's 1987 painting *Window X* captures the emotional and cultural isolation that is at the heart of Bâ's 1981 novel, *Scarlet Song.* In the novel, Mireille stands as a voyeur, an outsider peering into the innerworkings of a marriage she witnesses slowly fail.

able to face the challenges confronting women in African society. Ramatoulaye turns her confinement into a ritual of transformation by forgiving her husband, accepting his death, and discovering her own voice, as when she refuses two inappropriate suitors. In her handling of her pregnant daughter, she also provides a positive model of motherhood and stands in contrast to the mothers of both Mawdo and Binetou. By recounting all of these changes in her letter, Ramatoulaye performs her own *mirasse*, exposing the betrayals of her husband and of society, and writes herself into a new life.

SOURCES FOR FURTHER STUDY

Klaw, Barbara. "Mariama Bâ's *Une si longue lettre* and Subverting a Mythology of Sex-Based Oppression." *Research in African Literatures* 31, no. 2 (summer 2000): 132–147.

Pritchett, James A. "Mariama Bâ's *So Long a Letter.*" In *African Novels in the Classroom*, edited by Margaret Hay. Boulder, CO: Lynne Rienner, 2000, pp. 49–62.

Other Works

SCARLET SONG (1981). While betrayal leads to divorce and abandonment in *So Long a Letter,* it actually provokes insanity and assault in Mariama Bâ's second novel, *Scarlet Song*. This novel depicts the interracial marriage of a French woman named Mireille, the daughter of a diplomat, and a Senegalese man named Ousmane. They fall in love at school, but Mireille is taken back to France after her family learns of the relationship. They remain true to one another and marry in secrecy once Mireille converts to the Islamic faith. Afterward, they begin their married life together in Dakar. Both enter the marriage with the intention of remaining monogamous, but they prove unable to make the adjustments that a mixed-race union demands. Ousmane's extended family cannot tolerate Mireille, and he is gradually influenced by them to take an African woman as a second wife. Having rejected her family back in France, Mireille has no one to turn to when she learns of the betrayal and is completely destabilized by it. Unlike Ramatoulaye and Aissatou, she does not emerge from the betrayal a stronger person; rather, she loses her mental grounding, attacks her husband, and kills their child. It is not solely the cultural differences that destroy their marriage, for there are examples of successful mixed-race pairs in the novel. Rather, they fail in love because they are both unwilling to compromise, and as a result Ousmane is drawn to a cultural practice that an outsider like Mireille cannot ever understand or embrace.

Resources

Opportunities for further research into Mariama Bâ are somewhat limited, but the resources listed below are good places to start.

Africana Collection. This Web site, based at the University of Florida, provides contextual information on Mariama Bâ, as well as similar information about a broad spectrum of other African writers (http://web.uflib.ufl.edu/cm/africana/ba.htm).

Documentary. A film entitled *Femme aux yeux ouverts* (Women with Eyes Open) offers insight into and context for Mariama Bâ's writing, for it presents portraits of contemporary women from the West African countries of Burkina Faso, Mali, Senegal, and Benin. The women discuss their efforts to speak out and organize around five key issues: marital rights, reproductive health, female genital mutilation, the role of women in the economy, and the involvement of women in politics. This film is produced by Anne-Laure Folly and is available for rent or purchase from California Newsreel (www.newsreel.org.)

RENÉE T. SCHATTEMAN

Samuel Beckett

BORN: April 13, 1906, Foxrock, County Dublin, Ireland
DIED: December 22, 1989, Paris, France
IDENTIFICATION: Irish author whose avant-garde plays and novels explore the despair, pain, and comedy of the human condition.

SIGNIFICANCE: Samuel Beckett produced his most important work in France in the decades following World War II. A truly international author, Beckett wrote in French as well as English. His best-known play, *Waiting for Godot,* was written in French and first performed and published in Paris as *En attendant Godot* (1952). The play's darkly comic, antirealist depiction of two bored tramps awaiting the mysterious Godot—who never does arrive—won its author worldwide fame and helped revolutionize the mid-twentieth-century theater. This and other plays by Beckett are performed in many countries and languages, and his books are widely read and studied. Beckett was awarded the Nobel Prize for literature in 1969.

Samuel Barclay Beckett was born in Foxrock, a prosperous Dublin suburb, on April 13, 1906; he had one older brother, Frank. Beckett's father, William, was a successful quantity surveyor—a profession similar to being an architect. He married Maria (May) Roe in 1901 and in 1902 built the home, called Cooldrinagh after the country manor where May had grown up, in which Samuel was born.

Childhood in Ireland.
Samuel was a solitary, quiet child. William Beckett, a gregarious man of the world, often took his son on long, silent walks in the starkly beautiful Dublin mountains. The barren landscapes of Beckett's plays and fiction are recognizable versions of this lonely Irish countryside.

Beckett's relationship with his mother was at once loving and difficult. Both were exceedingly polite in company but privately given to spells of moodiness and depression. As Beckett grew older, he and his mother fought over what she saw as his unwillingness to take up a proper profession and what he saw as her inability to understand his artistic calling.

Schooling.
Beckett received a wholly conventional education for the son of well-to-do Irish Protestant parents. At the age of 14, he boarded at the Portora Royal School in the north of Ireland. Run along the lines of a traditional English public school, Portora emphasized sport

A typical Paris café in 1928. Beckett told a friend he wrote his first prose book in a café opposite the Luxembourg Gardens—possibly, his friend guessed, because he did not have the money to heat his apartment.

Trinity College in Dublin. His successor wrote that when Beckett lectured he "would stand for minutes staring through the window and then throw a perfectly constructed sentence to his crumb picking avid audience."

as much as academics. This arrangement suited Beckett well, since he was a natural athlete who excelled at swimming, cricket, and rugby.

In 1923 Beckett entered Trinity College, Dublin, pursuing a degree in modern languages. At first this "pursuit" was unenthusiastic—he preferred golfing and motoring to attending lectures. Eventually Beckett became more interested in his studies and won prizes and scholarships.

Teaching in Paris. In 1928 Beckett was appointed to an instructorship in English at France's premiere institution of higher education, the École Normale Supérieure in Paris, under an arrangement it had with Trinity College.

The two years he spent at the École Normale did little to encourage him toward an academic career, but Paris itself was a revelation. There he met the great Irish expatriate author James Joyce. Beckett became a part of Joyce's circle and helped the older Irish writer, whose eyesight had badly deteriorated, with his last great work, the novel *Finnegans Wake*. Beckett also helped translate part of the book into French and at Joyce's request wrote an essay in its defense.

The Young Writer. In Paris Beckett grew serious about becoming a writer. His award-winning poem *Whoroscope* was published as a single volume in 1930, and a critical book, written in English, on the French novelist Marcel Proust appeared in 1931.

In 1930 Beckett returned to Trinity as a lecturer in French. After Paris, though, Dublin seemed provincial and stifling. He took a master's degree in 1931 but then quit and spent the next decade living in Paris and London.

Beckett was having little success with his writing. In 1932 he wrote a novel, *Dream of*

Fair to Middling Women, which he could not get published. By cannibalizing the manuscript he produced a story collection, *More Pricks Than Kicks,* that was published in 1934 but did not sell well. In 1935 he began a new novel, *Murphy;* although it represented an advance, he was uncertain he was moving in the right artistic direction. Publishers agreed. It was rejected many times, and when it finally appeared in 1938, sales were dismal.

The War Years. Beckett was in Paris at the outbreak of World War II, and when France fell to the Germans, he joined the French Resistance. Beckett was mostly apolitical, but he often took stands against totalitarianism and bigotry, as he did against Nazism. After the war the French government awarded him the Croix de Guerre.

The "Siege in the Room." As Europe returned to normal, Beckett retreated to an apartment in Paris's Rue des Favorites, which he shared with his companion, Suzanne Deschevaux-Dumesnil (whom he married in 1961). Beckett would later call the years between 1946 and 1950 the "siege in the room," a time when he did little except write.

Writing in French, freed of inherited linguistic baggage and more able to express what he truly felt, he produced his great trilogy of novels. *Molloy* was completed in 1948, *Malone meurt (Malone Dies)* was finished the same year, and *L'innommable (The Unnamable)* was completed in 1950. His play *Waiting for Godot* was begun in October 1948 and finished in January 1949.

Success. Beckett emerged from the siege in the room exhausted; he also doubted he

would ever see any of what he had written appear publicly. It was largely left to Suzanne to find a publisher for the novels and a theater willing to put on the plays. When the firm Les Éditions de Minuit published the first two volumes of the trilogy in 1951 and the third in 1953, critical reaction was favorable, even enthusiastic. With even more spectacular results, *Godot* was first performed at the Théâtre de Babylone on January 5, 1953.

Although the play's unconventionality caused a great deal of confusion, it also created a great deal of excitement. Critics and audiences alike recognized that *Godot* heralded a new kind of theater and made a major cultural and philosophical statement. Somewhat to his

French villagers hang a Nazi effigy as a GI looks on. Beckett spent World War II in a village like this, fighting as part of the French Resistance.

HIGHLIGHTS IN BECKETT'S LIFE

1906   Samuel Barclay Beckett is born in Foxrock, County Dublin, Ireland.

1920   Attends the Portora Royal School.

1923–1927 Attends Trinity College, Dublin.

1928   Teaches at the École Normale Supérieure in Paris; meets James Joyce and helps him with *Finnegans Wake.*

1930   *Whoroscope* wins a literary prize, and the poem is published as a book.

1933   Beckett enters psychoanalysis in London.

1934   *More Pricks Than Kicks,* first prose fiction, is published.

1936–1937 Beckett is stabbed on a Paris street; while recovering, begins lifelong relationship with Suzanne Deschevaux-Dumesnil.

1938   Publishes *Murphy.*

1940–1941 Germans take Paris; Beckett joins the French Resistance.

1942–1944 In Roussillon, France, works on *Watt,* his last novel in English.

1945   Works as a Red Cross volunteer in Saint-Lô, France.

1946–1950 Finishes the trilogy of novels, *Waiting for Godot,* and other works, all in French (the "siege in the room" period).

1953   *Godot*'s debut in Paris gains Beckett international fame.

1957   Radio play, *All That Fall,* is performed on the BBC; *Endgame* is performed in London.

1958   *Krapp's Last Tape,* written in English, is performed in London.

1961   Beckett marries Suzanne Deschevaux-Dumesnil in England; *Happy Days* is performed in London.

1964–1965 Beckett travels to New York (his only U.S. visit) to produce his screenplay, *Film,* with the legendary actor Buster Keaton.

1969   Wins Nobel Prize.

1972   *Not I,* a monologue spoken by a disembodied mouth, debuts in New York.

1983   *Nacht und Träume (Night and Dream),* written for German television, is seen by two million viewers.

1986   Beckett is diagnosed with emphysema and confined to Paris nursing home; prose volume *Stirrings Still* appears; he writes last work, the poem "What Is the Word."

1989   Suzanne dies; Beckett dies in Paris on December 22 and is buried in Montparnasse cemetery.

Beckett, world-famous and entering old age. The writer, his publisher recalled, "was very convinced that the whole human experiment was a failure." He could play happily, however, with a friend's child. The actress Madeleine Renaud, after two months of rehearsing *Happy Days* with the author, found him a mystery. "Who knows Beckett?" she wrote. "Undoubtedly his wife does. But as for others, myself? I only know what he looks like."

as *Endgame*, which he began in 1955. The sadistic master-servant relationship at its core—not to mention that the two characters spend the entire play in trash cans—makes this perhaps his darkest work. It debuted in 1957 in London in the original French. Though reaction was even more mixed than it had been for *Godot, Endgame* is now considered a classic.

Beckett continued to experiment with the theater. In 1957 his radio play *All That Fall* was produced by the BBC; in 1958 he used the new technology of the tape recorder in *Krapp's Last Tape. Happy Days* (1961) ends with Winnie, its central character, buried up to her neck in a mound of dirt.

The Nobel Prize. A deeply reclusive person who loathed all forms of publicity, Beckett was horrified to learn he had won the Nobel Prize in 1969. The prize meant incessant requests for press interviews, which he was always reluctant to grant. He donated much of the prize money to other authors who were less financially successful than he himself was.

dismay, Beckett found he had become famous. This fame spread with the play's London debut in 1955 and its American premiere in Miami in 1956. Neither opening was free of controversy, but the derisive attacks and the passionate defenses it provoked only solidified its reputation.

Theatrical Experimentation. Beckett's next major play was *Fin de partie,* known in English

Final Years. Besides traveling to Europe to direct and supervise various productions of his plays, Beckett spent the final years of his life writing ever shorter plays and prose texts.

On July 17, 1989, Suzanne died. Beckett himself had already entered a nursing home not far from his apartment in the Boulevard Saint-Jacques. He passed away from respiratory failure on December 22, 1989, and was buried in Paris's Montparnasse cemetery.

Samuel Beckett's plays and fiction constitute an intense inquiry into the depths of the human condition, which Beckett considered appalling, lonely, and absurd. He constantly questions humans' folly and pretense, especially their simultaneously comic and futile attempts to make sense of their lives. For Beckett all claims to philosophical or artistic certainty are doomed to failure.

Still, his work is often very funny and usually deeply humane. No matter how awful the circumstances, Beckett implies, there is something oddly noble about the individual's drive to soldier on, however pointless or even pathetic the struggle might seem.

Literary Apprenticeship. Early in his career Beckett wrote poetry. *Whoroscope,* a poem about the French philosopher René Descartes, won a competition sponsored by the Hours Press, a small Paris-based company. Beckett earned about 10 pounds and saw the poem published as a separate volume.

Whoroscope is difficult to read. While it contains flashes of brilliance, it is densely packed with arcane allusions. Like much of his early

Beckett rehearses *Endgame* with members of Berlin's Schiller Theater in 1967. The troupe was his favorite in the years from the mid-1960s on, when he began directing his plays. Beckett's staging preferences could be fiendishly detailed—for *Happy Days* he diagrammed every move a character made during a sequence that could not be seen by the audience.

writing, it gives the impression of having been written by a gifted young intellectual showing off rather than by an artist speaking with an original voice.

Similar difficulties plagued his early fiction. He completed his first attempt at a novel in 1932, but *Dream of Fair to Middling Women* failed to attract a publisher and only appeared posthumously, in 1992. It is chiefly of value to students interested in excavating the origins of Beckett's mature work. Much the same could be said of the story collection that emerged from this novel's ruins, *More Pricks Than Kicks* (1934). Though published in Ireland—and then promptly banned by that country's overzealous censorship board—Beckett was unsatisfied with it.

Beckett's novel *Murphy* (1938) focuses on its supremely passive title character and his fondness for insane asylums and death. In its mordant humor and strangely grim lyricism,

Murphy approaches the style Beckett would later develop. Nevertheless, many critics rank it with his apprentice work.

The Revelation. Beckett claimed that, while on a visit to Ireland in 1946, he experienced a revelation. He saw that he had been proceeding in the wrong direction. He had been trying to be the all-knowing, stylistically dazzling artist capable of accurately representing and explaining the world to his readers. Now he would plumb the murkier depths of inner human reality. Instead of utilizing omniscient third-person narrators, Beckett would focus on characters who do not know the answers to such basic questions as who they are and what they are supposed to be doing.

Beckett and Modernism. To some degree the younger Beckett had been caught up in the

A friend who said Beckett thought "it would have been far better if the human race had never developed" also remembered his "selflessness and generosity" and his knack for lively conversation on depressing subjects. Most people reminiscing about Beckett "will tell you a lot about bars and restaurants and late-night drinking places," he wrote, "because that is really where Sam spent a great deal of his time and where most people met him."

Samuel Beckett became alienated from his homeland as he matured. Except in the north, Ireland became autonomous of Britain in 1922, but political independence did not lead to the independence of individualistic thinkers and artists. While Beckett is honored in Ireland now, for much of his lifetime his books were banned, and he saw Irish culture as narrow-minded and puritanical.

Still, Ireland profoundly affected Beckett's work. His characters sometimes utilize specifically Irish turns of phrase even when speaking in French. Also, the landscapes of Beckett's work are often recognizably Irish, even when ostensibly they may not be set anywhere specific at all. Like other great Irish writers, such as James Joyce, W. B. Yeats, J. M. Synge, and Kate O'Brien, Beckett maintained a complex relationship with the country of his birth. His affection for the land and its ordinary people mingled with an animosity toward the more xenophobic aspects of its culture.

Beckett's friend and exemplar James Joyce, whom he met in Paris in the 1920s, was an espe-cially significant influence upon Beckett. Their most fa-mous works are radically different. As Beckett himself suggested, Joyce tried to include everything in his art, while Beckett sought to keep everything out. Joyce's ca-reer began with short stories and ended with ambitiously long novels. Beckett's career proceeded in the opposite direction: he began with novels and ended with very short texts.

Still, Joyce was important to Beckett as a model of total artistic integrity. Joyce pursued his literary vision in the face of tremendous obstacles, including censorship and almost worldwide scorn. Beckett maintained his own in-tegrity as well as his respect for Joyce to the end of his life.

A 1935 portrait of James Joyce by artist Jacques Émile Blanche. The ex-tent of Beckett's involvement in Joyce's life and career is disputed by the various commentators of both legendary writers, but it is broadly ac-cepted that Joyce was a profound inspiration to Beckett. However, claiming that it was easier to write "without style" in French, Beckett de-veloped a style that could not have been more remote from Joyce's.

atmosphere of literary modernism. Broadly speaking, modernism sought to replace realism with more complex modes of artistic expression. Although there are crucial differences in the great English-language modernist authors, such as the poets T. S. Eliot and Ezra Pound and the novel-ist James Joyce, Beckett's friend and fellow Irishman, they share a willingness to experiment with traditional literary forms and an apparent impulse to re-create the totality of the human ex-perience in their art, even those parts of human life that realism cannot depict, such as dreams.

Beckett retained a fondness for the experi-mental. The lack of a clear plot in his plays and fiction challenged the belief that literature ought to describe something happening. It has been fa-mously observed of *Waiting for Godot* (1952) that in it nothing happens—*twice*. In *Molloy* (1951), the first volume of Beckett's trilogy, the title character struggles to visit his mother, but the narrative simply breaks off with the hapless Molloy lying in a ditch. Beckett abandoned the idea that stories should have a clear beginning and proceed to a definite ending.

However, Beckett distanced himself from the modernist attempt to account for the world in its entirety. His mission was to represent, as harrowingly as possible, primal states of doubt, solitude, and ignorance, as well as the deep human need to speak out about one's existence, even when one has nothing to say and would much rather be silent.

Writing in French.

One aspect of Beckett's revelation was his decision to write in French. Much of his best-known work, including *Godot* and the trilogy, was first written in French and subsequently translated into English, usually by Beckett himself. English was too richly loaded with literary and personal associations, and his early poetry and fiction in English are marred by excessive erudition. French permitted him to cut straight to the bone and helped him achieve a startling clarity and beautiful simplicity.

Beckett's Techniques and Characters.

In prose Beckett's mature technique employed first-person monologue. His narrators are typically physically decrepit men who disclaim any certain knowledge of how they have found themselves in the difficulties they describe and who have no idea how to extricate themselves from their various predicaments.

These narrators often suspect that they possess no other reality than that that exists by virtue of the human need to tell stories. In the last volume of his trilogy, *The Unnamable* (1953), especially, the "unnamable" narrator reveals that all the other narrators in the trilogy, such as Molloy and Malone, were no more than manifestations of his own storytelling drive. Beckett's fiction rests on this central paradox: human beings can say nothing for certain, even that they exist, yet are incapable of remaining silent.

In drama similarly confounded characters engage in endless bewildered dialogues or extended baffled soliloquies. In *Godot* the two chief characters, the tramps Vladimir and Estragon, cannot stop talking even when they have just loudly announced their intention of never speaking again. Neither are they capable of parting, despite their frequent assertions that they can no longer stand each other. Likewise, in *Endgame* Clov, the servant of the tyrannical Hamm, is never able to leave his appalling master, who himself cannot send Clov away forever.

Beckett's view of humanity in both his plays and his fiction is bleak but strangely sympathetic. Language is inadequate to express one's true self, yet people cannot refrain from speaking. Other people cannot fulfill one's own deepest longings and desires, but no one can do without companionship. The only things that make life's horrendous condition tolerable are humor—Beckett never stops joking, even as he describes the most squalid situations—and the ability to resolutely struggle on, even if for no other reason than that there is nothing else to do.

BIBLIOGRAPHY

Bair, Deirdre. *Samuel Beckett: A Biography.* New York: Summit, 1978.

Ben-Zvi, Linda. *Samuel Beckett.* Boston: Twayne, 1986.

Cohn, Ruby. *Just Play: Beckett's Theater.* Princeton, NJ: Princeton University Press, 1980.

Cronin, Anthony. *Samuel Beckett: The Last Modernist.* New York: HarperCollins, 1997.

Gordon, Lois. *The World of Samuel Beckett, 1906–1946.* New Haven, CT: Yale University Press, 1996.

Graver, Lawrence, and Raymond Federman, eds. *Samuel Beckett: The Critical Heritage.* London: Routledge, 1979.

Harrington, John P. *The Irish Beckett.* Syracuse, NY: Syracuse University Press, 1991.

Knowlson, James. *Damned to Fame: The Life of Samuel Beckett.* London: Bloomsbury, 1996.

McCarthy, Patrick A., ed. *Critical Essays on Samuel Beckett.* Boston: G. K. Hall, 1986.

O'Brien, Eoin. *The Beckett Country: Samuel Beckett's Ireland.* Dublin: Black Cat Press, 1986.

Pilling, John, ed. *The Cambridge Companion to Beckett.* New York: Cambridge University Press, 1994.

Reader's Guide to Major Works

WAITING FOR GODOT

Genre: Play
Subgenre: Tragicomedy
Published: Paris, 1952
Time period: None specified
Setting: A country road and a tree:
   no other details specified

Themes and Issues. *Waiting for Godot* was the first of Beckett's plays to be performed or published. It remains his signature work, the one for which he is best known. First performed in Paris in 1953, it has been in more or less ceaseless production for half a century and has been translated into dozens of languages.

Beckett wrote the play very rapidly, between October 1948 and January 1949. He later said that writing it preserved his sanity. He was in the midst of the "siege in the room" and deeply mired in the difficult labor required by his trilogy of novels; *Godot* offered him a release. Indeed, while some contemporary critics at-

A moment from the 1955 production in London that introduced *Waiting for Godot* to the English-speaking world. Pozzo (Peter Bull) orates, Lucky (Timothy Bateson) snoozes, and Vladimir (Paul Daneman) and Estragon (Peter Woodthorpe) listen. *The Sunday Times*'s Harold Hobson accused his fellow critics of showering "bat-blind abuse" on the play. Audiences also had their doubts, he wrote later, with almost every performance of its six-month run suffering occasional outbursts from "malcontents." One of these might have been Beckett. A friend recalled watching the production with Beckett clutching his arm "and in a clearly heard stage whisper saying: 'It's ahl wrahng! He's doing it ahl wrahng!'"

tacked it for its pessimism, it remains for many readers and viewers one of the funniest of all of Beckett's works. Beckett called the play a tragicomedy, since it depicts tragedy and comedy as inextricably combined aspects of the human condition.

In *Godot* Beckett set himself several goals. He was determined to dispense with the obstacles presented by artistic realism. Although the play was written in French and the script retains many Irishisms, the country road on which the action takes place could be any country road anywhere. This universality is important because it allows Beckett to zero in on his main purpose: to represent the total inability of human beings to know why they are placed upon this earth at all and to act out their constant inquiries into the question of why it is

they must suffer while they are here. Beckett's intention was to stage a state of doubt and uncertainty fundamental to the human condition.

The Plot. Strictly speaking, *Waiting for Godot* has no plot as such, if the term *plot* is understood as a sequence of significant events leading up to a clear conclusion. Nothing "happens" in any conventional dramatic sense in the play. In *Godot* Beckett makes the theatrically daring choice to explore simple boredom as one of his major themes.

The main characters are two tramps, Vladimir and Estragon. Estragon refers to Vladimir as Didi, and Vladimir refers to Estragon as Gogo. Very little of their backgrounds is revealed besides the fact that they have been together for a long time. They are

---

FICTION

1934	More Pricks Than Kicks
1938	Murphy
1951	Molloy
1951	Malone meurt (Malone Dies)
1953	L'innommable (The Unnamable)
1953	Watt
1955	Nouvelles et textes pour rien (Stories and Texts for Nothing)
1964	Comment c'est (How It Is)
1965	Imagination morte imaginez (Imagination Dead Imagine
1967	No's Knife: Collected Shorter Prose, 1945–1966.
1969	Sans (Lessness)
1970	Mercier et Camier (Mercier and Camier)
1970	Premier amour (First Love and Other Stories)
1970	Le depeupleur (The Lost Ones)
1976	All Strange Away
1976	Pour finir encore et autres foirades (Fizzles)
1980	Company
1981	Mal vu mal dit (Ill Seen Ill Said)
1983	Worstward Ho
1986	Stirrings Still
1988	As the Story Was Told
1992	Dream of Fair to Middling Women

PLAYS

1952	En attendant Godot (Waiting for Godot)
1957	All That Fall
1958	Fin de partie (Endgame)
1959	Krapp's Last Tape
1960	Embers
1961	Happy Days
1964	Play
1973	Not I
1976	Footfalls
1982	Rockaby
1984	What Where
1996	Eleutheria

FILM

1969	Film

POETRY

1930	Whoroscope
1935	Echo's Bones and Other Precipitates
1961	Poems in English
1984	Collected Poems 1930–1978

CRITICISM

1931	Proust
1983	Disjecta: Miscellaneous Writings and a Dramatic Fragment

clearly based upon vaudeville-era comedy teams, such as Laurel and Hardy, complete with bowler hats. Much of their dialogue reads like an old-fashioned comedy routine, and much of the action recalls standard vaudeville gags.

Didi and Gogo are literally waiting for Godot. Precisely who Godot is is never made clear, nor can the pair quite recall why they are waiting for him. All they seem to know for sure is that they were instructed to wait by the tree. While they wait, they tell each other stories to pass the time. They also squabble incessantly, discuss the benefits and drawbacks of killing themselves, and frequently threaten to get up and leave, though neither one manages to actually go.

Halfway through Act 1 another odd pair, Lucky and Pozzo, is introduced. Pozzo is a pompous and self-righteous master, and Lucky is his burden-carrying, silent slave. Lucky has a rope tied around his neck, and Pozzo drives him with a whip. Pozzo makes Lucky dance for the amusement of Gogo and Didi; when this entertainment does not work out very well, Lucky is ordered to think. When his hat is placed upon his head, he does so, uttering a stream of learned nonsense that only stops when his hat is forcibly removed by the other characters. After Lucky and Pozzo depart, a boy arrives to tell Gogo and Didi that Godot cannot come that evening but surely will tomorrow.

Act 2 takes place the next day. Four or five leaves have appeared on the tree, but little else has changed. Didi sings a repetitious song about a dead dog, and he and Gogo try to remember what they did the day before, even to the point of acting out their encounter with Lucky and Pozzo. Mostly they desperately try to pass the time. Lucky and Pozzo reappear.

A sympathetic agent suggested *Waiting for Godot* just might work in America as a vehicle for Bob Hope and Jack Benny. Decades later Robin Williams (left) and Steve Martin took on Estragon and Vladimir, respectively, in a 1989 production at Lincoln Center in New York. The play may have "knocked the shackles of plot from off the English drama," as Harold Hobson wrote, but it is also a good showcase for comedians who know how to milk a scene.

Pozzo, who has gone blind, falls and brings down Lucky with him, all their baggage in turn being scattered. He cries to Didi and Gogo for help, which they only render him after much debate. Eventually Pozzo regains his feet and his whip and again drives Lucky from the stage.

The boy reappears and once more tells the tramps that Godot will not be coming but will come tomorrow without fail. After the boy departs, Gogo tries to hang himself with the cord he uses as a belt with the sole effect of making his trousers fall down around his ankles. The play ends with Vladimir asking Estragon, "Well? Shall we go?" Estragon replies, "Yes, let's go." They do not move, and the curtain falls.

Analysis. Much critical ink has been spilled trying to explain the "meaning" of *Waiting for Godot*. It was widely assumed at the time of its first productions that the play was allegorical, that is, that the characters and their situation symbolized something else.

Usually, Godot was taken to be God. Vladimir, Estragon, Pozzo, and Lucky were thought of as representations of various types of human beings. Pozzo, for instance, would stand in for political despots of all kinds, and Lucky would stand for the people such despots crush beneath them. This allegorical approach to the play seems to be strengthened by the pronunciation that Beckett insisted upon for Godot: "*God*-oh."

However, Beckett always resisted allegorical interpretations of his work, especially as they were applied to *Godot*. The difficulty of this kind of an approach is that allegorical answers to the problems posed by the play are too simplistic. The point of the play is that people do not have any answers at all to the problems that beset them.

Beckett's view may be stated as follows: We cannot say for certain why we exist or that we are meant to do anything more while we are alive than pass the time as we wait for death. Great cruelty exists in the world, as seen in the harsh treatment the mute Lucky receives at the hands of Pozzo. Terrible things happen with-

out any real explanation: Pozzo is suddenly blind. Meanwhile, we wait for answers and enlightenment that may never be forthcoming, as Didi and Gogo wait for the eternally deferred arrival of Godot.

Still, Beckett seems to imply that at least people are not alone in their loneliness and ignorance. Estragon and Vladimir have each other—someone with whom they can pass the time and in whom they can find comfort. Though the play is unsparing in its depiction of savagery and doubt, it is also rich in humor, compassion, and humanity.

SOURCES FOR FURTHER STUDY

Astro, Alan. *Understanding Samuel Beckett*. Columbia: University of South Carolina Press, 1990.

Cousineau, Thomas. *Waiting for Godot: Form in Movement*. New York: Twayne, 1990.

Fletcher, Beryl S., and John Fletcher. *A Student's Guide to the Plays of Samuel Beckett*. 2nd ed. London: Faber, 1985.

McMillan, Dougald, and Martha Fehsenfeld. *Beckett in the Theatre: The Author as Practical Playwright and Director*. Vol. 1, *From "Waiting for Godot" to "Krapp's Last Tape."* New York: Riverrun, 1988.

Mercier, Vivian. *Beckett/Beckett*. New York: Oxford University Press, 1977.

THE TRILOGY: MOLLOY; MALONE DIES; THE UNNAMABLE

Genre: Novel
Subgenre: Avant-garde fiction
Published: Paris, 1951; 1951; 1953
Time period: None specified
Setting: None specified

Themes and Issues. If *Waiting for Godot* is Beckett's best-known work among the general public, his great trilogy of novels—*Molloy, Malone Dies,* and *The Unnamable*—is considered equally significant among literary scholars and Beckett devotees. It is widely held that the trilogy constitutes a reinvention of the novel that is every bit as profound as Beckett's reinvention of the theater in *Godot*.

Beckett spent years attempting to achieve his authentic voice in prose. His earlier novels in

English, especially *Murphy* and *Watt,* approach this voice in many ways, but it is perhaps only fully realized in the trilogy, which was written in French during the "siege in the room." The impact of this voice is nothing less than startling. Throughout the trilogy progressively deeper layers of novelistic conventions are stripped away to reveal a powerful emotional core and a complex meditation upon the nature of storytelling itself.

The trilogy is written from the perspective of a series of first-person narrators, beginning with Molloy and ending with the Unnamable. These narratives are challenging to read. The challenge lies not in understanding Beckett's language, which is usually quite clear. Rather, it lies in Beckett's refusal to provide the sort of information or structure that readers have historically come to expect of a novel. The narrators begin their stories abruptly and end them without having achieved any definite objective. No real background is provided for the characters. All the reader knows of them is what they choose to tell, and sometimes they deny knowing anything certain about themselves at all.

Moreover, the trilogy becomes increasingly metafictive. That is, the narrators become increasingly conscious that they are invented characters in a novel. Each narrator seems to exhibit a deeper reality than the one before so that reading the trilogy becomes something like peeling an onion (to use one of Beckett's favorite metaphors). At the end (or perhaps the center) is the Unnamable, the "I" who appears to be ultimately responsible for all the stories. The Unnamable is perhaps a representation of the primal human storytelling urge, the urge to take on the hopeless task of making sense of existence.

The Plot. Almost any attempt to summarize what happens in the trilogy is in some sense an exercise in futility because of Beckett's use of the trilogy to critique the notion that novels need a plot at all. However, a brief sketch may be presented.

The first long section of *Molloy* is told by its eponymous narrator, whose lame leg makes walking without crutches almost impossible but who nevertheless manages to use a bicycle. Molloy's story seems to be that of his journey to his mother's home, but he takes up this story at an arbitrary starting point and ends it with his decision to stay in a ditch at the edge of an unnamed forest. The other section is narrated by Moran, a secret agent of some sort ordered to make a report on Molloy. Molloy is not found, and the report is not made.

Malone Dies focuses upon the dying title character, who lies alone in his bed and tells stories, his own and those of people he invents, such as the boy Saposcat, or Sapo, who turns into an old man named Macmann. *The Unnamable,* the most difficult book in the trilogy, is narrated by its title character, who ap-

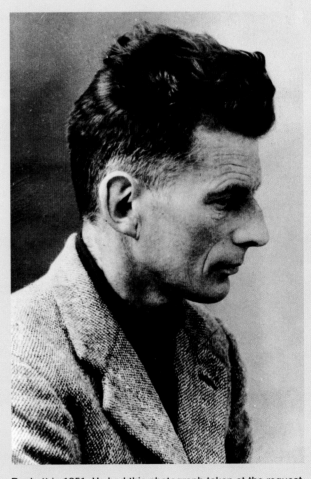

Beckett in 1951. He had this photograph taken at the request of *Molloy's* publisher; for years it was thought to be the only photo of him before he became famous. Beckett's wife said he came home depressed from meeting the publisher because he was convinced that *Molloy* would cause the firm to go bankrupt.

pears to exist in a jar, totally immobile. This speaker seems to admit to being the inventor of Molloy and Malone, along with Beckett's earlier antihero Murphy and some new figures named Basil, Mahood, and Worm. Eventually the narrative coalesces into a single, enormously long sentence, an uninterrupted gush of intense language.

Analysis. The trilogy is not easy to get through, but reading it attentively offers distinct rewards. Like much of Beckett's work, it is full of a mordant humor that can be strikingly funny. It is difficult to take one's own physical complaints too seriously after absorbing the comically elaborate lamentations of Molloy or Moran.

Beyond these considerations, the trilogy makes the careful reader sharply aware of the flimsiness of standard narrative conventions, which are so often taken for granted. For all its antirealism, the trilogy somehow feels more true to life than the average best-seller. Real life, after all, rarely provides easy answers or tidy resolutions. More often, real life really is as confusing as it is to Beckett's narrators, who consistently declare that they do not know how they came to be who or where they are.

Finally, although the trilogy is without doubt dark and grim in many places and almost excruciatingly dense in others, it is still shot through with a humanizing lyricism. *The Unnamable* ends with one of the most famous passages in all of modern literature: "I don't know, I'll never know, in the silence you don't know, you must go on, I can't go on, I'll go on." What the Unnamable will continue to do is to speak, to obey the mysterious yet imperative impulse to speak out about one's existence. It is, Beckett seems to suggest, this very impulse that most fully defines what it is to be human.

SOURCES FOR FURTHER STUDY

Alvarez, A. *Beckett*. London: Fontana, 1992.

Fletcher, John. *Samuel Beckett's Art*. London: Chatto and Windus, 1967.

Hill, Leslie. *Beckett's Fiction in Different Worlds*. Cambridge: Cambridge University Press, 1990.

Levy, Eric P. *Beckett and the Voice of Species: A Study of the Prose Fiction*. Totowa, NJ: Barnes and Noble, 1980.

Webb, Eugene. *Samuel Beckett: A Study of His Novels*. London: Peter Owen, 1970.

Other Works

ENDGAME (1958). *Endgame* was first performed at the Royal Court Theatre in London on April 3, 1957. Critics and audiences were baffled by it and not only because it was performed in French. Like all of Beckett's work, *Endgame* radically breaks with conventional forms so that, once again, there is no plot. Also, this play is decidedly grim. In the original rehearsals Beckett stressed to the actors that their lines should be read without any attempt to make them light or humorous.

The situation depicted in *Endgame* is bizarre to say the least. The action is set in a drab room inhabited by the blind and crippled Hamm and his truculent servant, Clov. Hamm's parents, Nagg and Nell, live in trash cans set up at the front of the stage. Hamm is domineering and cruel, while Clov is maltreated and spiteful. Nagg and Nell periodically pop up out of their bins to comment or complain; they are constant targets of Hamm's abuse. The world outside the room seems desolate. It is as if some great disaster has occurred to humanity, and only these four characters are left.

Beckett once suggested that Hamm and Clov were in some ways like Vladimir and Estragon from *Waiting for Godot* grown old. The chief similarity between the two pairs of characters seems to be that, like Didi and Gogo, Hamm and Clov are interdependent. Though they say they wish to leave each other, it is inconceivable that they ever will. In *Endgame,* however, the interdependence is far more bitter. Hamm cannot survive without Clov, so his cruelty is

Nell, played by Nydia Westman, and Nagg, played by P. J. Kelly, peep from their garbage cans in a 1958 production of *Endgame*. "NELL: Nothing is funnier than unhappiness, I grant you that. But—NAGG: [*Shocked.*] Oh! NELL: Yes, yes it's the most comical thing in the world. And we laugh, we laugh, with a will, in the beginning. But it's always the same thing. Yes, it's like the funny story we have heard too often, we still find it funny, but we don't laugh any more."

tempered with manipulation in order to make him stay. Clov desperately wishes to escape but knows there is nowhere for him to go.

In chess the endgame is the final stage before one of the players is finally defeated. In this play the characters execute increasingly frantic moves in order to stave off their inevitable doom. *Endgame* is thus bleaker and more terrifying than *Godot*. In the earlier play companionship relieved the boredom and the misery of the characters. In the later work companionship serves only to make matters worse.

KRAPP'S LAST TAPE (1959). *Krapp's Last Tape* debuted on October 28, 1958, at London's Royal Court Theatre, in English. *Krapp's Last Tape* is in some ways an autobio-

graphical piece; most memorably, Beckett's artistic revelation is recounted in it, albeit in disguised form.

The setting of the play is simple but ingenious. Krapp, an old man, is alone in a dark and cluttered room. For decades apparently he has been making tape recordings in which he describes his life—a sort of audio diary. On this particular evening he eats a banana and occasionally retires to the rear of the stage for a drink while he listens to his past selves speak to him of his life. Eventually he comes to a tape recounting a past love affair that he broke off. He finally makes a new tape, a fragmentary and embittered speech in which his current existence and his memories intermingle.

Krapp's Last Tape is one of Beckett's most accessible and emotional plays. The use of the tape recorder enables Beckett to represent on stage the paradoxical ways in which people remember their past. Like Krapp, the audience members are contemptuous of their former pomposities and naïveté yet at the same time are envious of the people they once were, before whom, in retrospect, endless possibilities for happiness might have opened up, if only they had known it at the time.

Resources

Collections of Samuel Beckett's manuscripts and other Beckett material are held by the Harry Ransom Humanities Research Center at the University of Texas at Austin, Dartmouth University Library, and the Burns Library of Boston College. The largest collection of such materials is in the Beckett Collection at Reading University, England. Important collections are also held by Trinity College, Dublin, and the Archives de Paris. Other resources are as follows:

The Beckett International Foundation is a charitable trust administered by Reading University, England. Information about the catalog of the Beckett Archive, as well as about requesting permissions from Beckett's estate for the purpose of staging his plays, may be found at its Web site (http://www.rdg.ac.uk/libweb/Lib/Bif/bif.html).

Journal of Beckett Studies. This academic journal is published by the English department of Florida State University. Its Web site lists the contents of current and past issues (www.english.fsu.edu/jobs/default.cfm).

Samuel Beckett Online Resources and Links Page. This site is a very comprehensive resource (http://home.sprintmail.com/~lifeform/Beck_Links.html).

Samuel Beckett Society. This organization of scholars, students, directors, and actors discusses and promotes the study and performance of Samuel Beckett's works. The society publishes *The Beckett Circle,* a biannual newsletter. It maintains an excellent Web site that provides basic as well as academic resources (http://beckett.english.ucsb.edu).

ANDREW HAGGERTY

Jorge Luis Borges

BORN: August 24, 1899, Buenos Aires, Argentina
DIED: June 14, 1986, Geneva, Switzerland
IDENTIFICATION: Esteemed Argentinian author of short stories, poems, and essays who is renowned for his erudition, his metaphysical musings, and his fanciful imagination.

SIGNIFICANCE: Although Jorge Luis Borges was educated in Europe and immersed from earliest youth in the literary traditions of England and North America, he is considered the most important predecessor of the so-called boom period in Latin American literature, which began in the decade of the 1960s. His work—mostly poetry in the 1920s and 1930s, then short fiction in the 1940s—brought him recognition from around the globe. Despite many health problems, particularly with his eyesight, Borges traveled the world over. In addition, he collaborated with other important writers (such as Adolfo Bioy Casares), worked on several literary reviews, and wrote valuable works of biography, cultural studies, and literary criticism.

On August 24, 1899, Jorge Luis Borges was born in Buenos Aires, Argentina. His parents, Jorge and Leonor, were living in the bride's parents' home at the time. The family later moved from this house in the center of the city to a suburb of Buenos Aires known as Palermo. This rough neighborhood would later become the subject of many of Borges's writings.

Childhood. Nicknamed Georgie by his parents, the young Borges was surrounded from birth with the English language and culture that his father loved. In fact, Georgie's first words were in English, not the Spanish of his native land. His first books were English as well. He began reading at a young age, around four, but did not attend school until age nine. By that time Georgie had already written some pieces in English and translated others from English to Spanish.

Education and Travels as a Youth. In 1914 the family moved to Geneva, Switzerland, in search of a cure for the elder Jorge's poor eye-

A horse and carriage can be spotted in the traffic at the Diagonal Norte of Buenos Aires. When his family returned to Argentina in 1921, Borges wrote, he was startled to find how Buenos Aires had grown. He loved exploring it and remembered the place as a "very kindly city" dominated by patios and flat roofs, a place where everyone knew each other. The metropolis of recent decades was unrecognizable to him. "I'm 84," he said, "and at my age one is a stranger in one's own land."

sight. Here Georgie began his studies in French. He was an avid reader from his youth, a characteristic that would last his entire life, as did his love for travel. The young Borges came into contact with many intellectuals and writers of the time, particularly after 1919, when the family relocated to Spain.

Borges the Writer and Scholar. Borges returned to his home in Buenos Aires in 1921, fresh from the literary circles of Europe, and immediately set about writing poetry and essays, collaborating in literary reviews, and meeting his contemporaries from throughout Latin America. By 1923 his first two books had been published, *Fervor de Buenos Aires (Fervor of Buenos Aires)* and *Poemas (Poems)*. That same year the family would return to Geneva for his father's eye surgery.

Back in Buenos Aires, Borges continued to write and publish poetry and essays. In 1937, nearing the age of 40, he got his first paying job, a post at a municipal library. This job lasted until Juan Perón was elected president of Argentina in 1946. Several events that occurred during these years at the library became turning points for Borges. His father passed away in 1938, and after an accident in a stairway that same year, Borges contracted septicemia and was near death. This incident gave the writer inspiration for one of his first short stories, "El Sur" ("The South"). For much of the next two decades, Borges's attention would be turned to the short story and metaphysics. In 1941 a collection of stories, *El jardín de senderos que se bifurcan (The Garden of Forking Paths)* was published, followed in 1944 by another, *Ficciones* (Fictions; the English translation keeps the original Spanish title). *El Aleph (The Aleph)* appeared in 1949

FILMS BASED ON BORGES'S STORIES

1954 *Días del odio* (Day of hate)

1957 *Hombre de la esquina rosada* (The street-corner man)

1969 *Emma Zunz*

1970 *La strategia de la ragna* (The strategy of the spider)

1975 *El muerto cacique Bandeira*

1980 *La intrusa* (The intruder)

1992 *Historia del guerrero y la cautiva* (The story of the warrior and the captive woman)

Borges in 1943. As a writer he was esteemed by young intellectuals and ignored by just about everyone else. To survive he worked at a branch of the municipal library for "nine years of solid unhappiness." The other men concentrated on "horse racing, soccer matches, and smutty stories," he recalled. "I remember a fellow employee's noting in an encyclopedia the name of a certain Jorge Luis Borges—a fact that set him wondering at the coincidence of our identical names and birth dates."

HIGHLIGHTS IN BORGES'S LIFE

1899 Jorge Luis Borges is born in Buenos Aires on August 24.

1914 Travels to Europe with his family, settling in Geneva, where his father would receive treatment for problems with his eyesight.

1918 Family moves to Lugano.

1919 Family moves to Spain, first to Mallorca, later to Seville and Madrid.

1921 Borges returns to Buenos Aires; founds literary review *Prisma;* shares ideas gathered from his literary contacts in Europe, particularly the literary movement *ultraismo.*

1922 The literary review *Proa* is founded by a group of writers, including Borges.

1923 *Fervor of Buenos Aires* is published; Borges again travels with his family to Europe for his father's eye operation.

1926 *Proa* closes.

1931 Has first encounter with Adolfo Bioy Casares, his frequent collaborator; the literary review *Sur* first appears.

1937 Borges takes job at municipal library in Buenos Aires.

1938 His father dies (February 24).

1938 Borges contracts septicemia in head wound and nearly dies; incident becomes a turning point in his writing.

1946 Juan Perón is elected president of Argentina; Borges loses library post almost immediately.

1954 After eight eye operations, Borges is warned of imminent blindness.

1955 Juan Perón is deposed; Borges is named director of the National Library.

1961 Begins a literary collaboration with María Esther Vázquez; is awarded the Formentor Prize.

1963 Returns to Europe for first time since his youth.

1968 Begins collaboration with Norman Thomas di Giovanni, an American professor.

1973 Once more leaves the National Library.

1975 His mother dies.

1986 Borges marries María Kodama; dies in Switzerland on June 14.

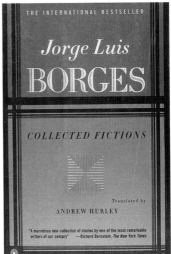

Borges receives an honorary doctorate at Oxford University in 1971. For him a high point of the visit was meeting Richard Hamer, a young scholar whose translations from Anglo-Saxon Borges admired. At the reception Borges spent almost an hour questioning his new friend about fine points of Anglo-Saxon meter and pronunciation.

much the result of his fame as a writer, both in Argentina and abroad. It was also possible because Juan Perón, Borges's political nemesis, had been forced out of office.

Awards and Travels. In the 1960s Borges began a series of collaborations with other authors, and he also returned to Europe for the first time since his youth. By 1970 his fame had grown to such a point that he was considered the favorite for the Nobel Prize for literature that year, but for partly political reasons the award went to Alexandr Solzhenitsyn. Borges also traveled to the United States and around the world, teaching at universities, receiving awards and honorary doctorates, and staying active in literary circles despite his age and health. He received honorary doctorates from Oxford University (1970), Columbia University (1971), the Sorbonne (1977), Harvard University (1981), Tokyo University (1984), and the universities of Palermo, Venice, and Rome (also 1984).

Last Years. Borges left the directorship of the National Library in 1973, just a month before Juan Perón assumed the presidency again after 18 years of exile, mostly in Spain under the Franco regime. Perón's death in 1974, which for Borges came "30 years too late," and the death of Borges's mother, with whom Borges had lived most of his life, were significant events of those years. Borges married a former student, María Kodama, just weeks before his death in Geneva in 1986 (though he was actually still legally married to Elsa Astete Millán, whom he had wed in 1967).

and, in 1951, *La muerte y la brújula (Death and the Compass)*. These are the books for which Borges became best known, and the stories they contain were widely translated and anthologized.

By 1954 Borges, like his father and in spite of eight surgical procedures over the years, was almost totally blind. Nevertheless, in 1955 he was named director of the National Library in Buenos Aires. This appointment was very

The Writer's Work

The works of Jorge Luis Borges fall into three main categories: poetry, which he wrote mainly (though not exclusively) as a young man in the 1920s; essays and other nonfiction works, endeavors he continued throughout his life; and short stories, written mainly in the 1940s and 1950s, the works for which he became most recognized.

Ultraismo—the Search for the Beyond.

The poetry of Borges in the early 1920s was influenced by the ultraist movement that had appeared in Spain during his stay there.

Borges in 1971, when overflow crowds at universities and literary conferences around the world listened to the man who once had been too shy to read his own lectures. His friend and biographer Emir Rodriguez Monegal wrote that Borges loved being famous and that audiences were "literally spaced out by his words, by the incantatory way in which he delivered them, by his blindness and his almost uncanny face."

Ultraismo, like futurism and dadaism, other literary movements in Europe at the time, was a call to modernization and revolution in language and literature, an attempt to take Spanish literature beyond the provincialism and conventionalism of writers of that time—hence the ultraism, the "beyondness," that the ultraist writers sought. By the time *Fervor of Buenos Aires* (sometimes translated as "Passion for Buenos Aires"), was published, however, Borges was again back in Argentina, and as the title suggests, the young man was very much enamored of his native land, despite his enduring fondness for the places and people of Europe. Borges was also inspired by a young woman he had met in Palermo, Concepción Guerrero, to whom he became engaged. The book of poems, still a favorite in Argentina because of its pride of place, showed the Buenos Aires of the *arrabales,* the poor neighborhoods of the city, reflected in the beauty and passion of his beloved Concepción.

Criollismo—a Turning Inward.

After the ultraist movement lost its impetus both in Europe and Argentina and after another trip to Switzerland for his father's eye operation, which effectively ended his engagement to Concepción Guerrero, Borges adopted an intense nationalism in his writing and embraced a movement that would come to be called *criollismo* (the best translation of *criollo* as used by the residents of Buenos Aires is "native Argentine"). Two works of the time were especially indicative of this trend: in 1926 *El*

The tomb of Eva Perón, wife of dictator Juan Domingo Perón and a power in his regime. To Borges she was a "streetwalker" and her husband a "second-rater," and he told the press so when Perón returned to power in 1973. The writer could accept dictatorship, but he considered Perónism to be the same as Nazism. In the 1940s the view cost him his library post, an ouster that took the form of a mocking "promotion" to inspector of chickens and rabbits—both symbols of cowardice. In the 1970s Borges and his aged mother stood off Perónist death threats. She told an anonymous caller he would have to hurry because she was 98.

tamaño de mi esperanza (The measure of my hope) and in 1928 *El idioma de los argentinos* (The language of the Argentines), both collections of essays on the Argentine character and the peculiarities of Argentinian Spanish.

The Move to Fiction. Several important events in the life of Borges occurred in the late 1930s. His appointment to a post in the municipal library of Buenos Aires in 1937 gave him a steady income and access to the library's collection for his own studies. His thirst for knowledge and his mastery of English, French, and German, plus some familiarity with Latin and Hebrew, made Borges a formidable scholar. In 1938 Borges's father died, blind and in poor health. At the end of 1938, on Christmas Eve, as he ran up a flight of stairs, Borges, suffering from the poor eyesight he inherited from his father, struck a window he did not see; the resulting wound on his head, imbedded with fragments of glass, became infected, and Borges fell gravely ill. His fevered hallucinations became the inspiration of one of his first short stories, "The

South." Borges's wide-ranging scholarship was also displayed in the stories that followed.

The Short Stories. After the Argentinian focus of his poetry and essays, Borges's short stories, characterized by universal themes both in subject matter and in the language used, were bound to surprise his readers. The profound erudition displayed, the metaphysical topics addressed, and the fanciful imagination contained there constituted an intellectual challenge to anyone who read them, and yet, through humor and self-conscious narrative techniques, the stories attracted a global following for Borges. These are the works for which Borges is most recognized.

BIBLIOGRAPHY

Alazraki, Jaime. *Borges and the Kabbalah.* Cambridge, UK: Cambridge University Press, 1988.

Balderston, Daniel. *The Literary Universe of Jorge Luis Borges. An Index to References and Allusions to Persons, Titles, and Places in His Writings.* Westport, CT: Greenwood Press, 1986.

The sign reads "Long Live the Fatherland" and shows the Argentine flag alongside a cartoon about "The Dreams of Uncle Sam—And Dreams the Dreams Are." Borges dabbled early on with literary nativism, but he appreciated universal values and admired foreign powers—notably Britain, the United States, and Israel—far too much to fit in with nationalists or the Left. Above all he detested propaganda. "I believe in revolution," he said, but he added that it was one without flags. "When they tell of some new revolution I always ask 'and do they have a flag?' and when they say 'yes,' I know that it is not my revolution."

POETRY

1923   Fervor of Buenos Aires
1925   Luna de enfrente (The moon in front)
1929   Cuaderno San Martín
1943   Poemas
1958   Poemas
1964   Obra poética (Poetic works)
1969   El otro, el mismo (The other, the same)
1975   La rosa profunda (The unending rose)
1976   La moneda de hierro (The iron coin)
1977   Historia de la noche (History of the night)
1981   La cifra (The cipher)

SHORT STORY COLLECTIONS

1935   Historia universal de la infamia (A Universal History of Infamy)
1941   The Garden of Forking Paths
1944   Ficciones
1949   The Aleph
1951   Death and the Compass
1970   El informe de Brodie (Doctor Brodie's Report)
1975   El libro de arena (The Book of Sand)
1977   Rosa y azul (Rose and blue)
1983   23 agosto 1983 y otros cuentos (August 23, 1983, and other stories)

SCREENPLAYS (WITH ALFREDO BIOY CASARES)

1968   Invasión (Invasion)
1974   Les autres (The others)
1975   Los orilleros

ESSAY COLLECTIONS

1925   Inquisiciones (Inquisitions)
1926   El tamaño de mi esperanza (The measure of my hope)
1928   El idioma de los argentinos (The language of the Argentines)
1932   Discusión (Discussion)
1935   Historia de la eternidad (History of eternity)
1952   Otras inquisiciones (Other Inquisitions)
1975   Prólogos (Prologues)
1980   Siete noches (Seven Nights)
1982   Nuevos ensayos dantescos

MISCELLANEOUS WORKS

1930   Evaristo Carriego (biography)
1960   El hacedor (Dreamtigers) (poems and prose)
1961   Una antología personal (A Personal Anthology) (poems, prose, essays)
1965   Para las seis cuerdas (For six strings) (song lyrics)
1969   Elogio de la sombra (Praise of the shade) (poems and prose)
1972   El oro de los tigres (The Gold of the Tigers) (poems and prose poems)
1979   Obras completas en colaboración (works done in collaboration with other authors)
1985   Los conjurados (The conjured) (poems and prose)
1986   Textos cautivos (articles from El Hogar)

Barnstone, Willis. *With Borges on an Ordinary Evening in Buenos Aires.* Chicago: University of Illinois Press, 1993.

Barnstone, Willis, et al.. *Borges at Eighty: Conversations.* Champaign: University of Indiana Press, 1982.

Barrenechea, Ana. *Borges the Labyrinth Maker.* New York: New York University Press, 1965.

Burgin, Richard. *Conversations with Jorge Luis Borges.* London: Souvenir Press, 1973.

Christ, Ronald. *The Narrow Act: Borges's Art of Allusion.* New York: New York University Press, 1969.

Cohen, J. M. *Jorge Luis Borges.* Edinburgh: Oliver and Boyd, 1973.

Di Giovanni, Norman Thomas, ed. *The Borges Tradition.* London: Constable, 1995.

—-. *In Memory of Borges.* London: Constable, 1988.

Merrell, Floyd. *Unthinking Thinking: Jorge Luis Borges, Mathematics and the New Physics.* West Lafayette, IN: Purdue University Press, 1991.

Molloy, Sylvia. *Signs of Borges.* Durham, NC: Duke University Press, 1994.

Sarlo, Beatriz. *Jorge Luis Borges: The Writer on the Edge.* London: Verso, 1993.

Sturrock, John. *Paper Tigers: The Ideal Fictions of Jorge Luis Borges.* New York: Oxford University Press, 1978.

Borges in Collaboration with Other Writers

A notable feature of Jorge Luis Borges's literary career was his collaboration with other writers throughout his life. Even though he suffered from poor eyesight from a very young age, Borges traveled the world over. In his travels and studies abroad, Borges was always in contact with the literary circles and important figures of the places he visited and lived. He collaborated with such important writers as Adolfo Bioy Casares, Alfonso Reyes, and Pedro Henríquez Ureña, founded and worked on several literary reviews, and wrote valuable works of biography, cultural studies, and literary criticism.

The first published work by Jorge Luis Borges was a translation into Spanish of Oscar Wilde's "The Happy Prince" in 1909, which he wrote at the age of nine. The translation was possible because of Borges's education and upbringing in the English language, as well as the Spanish of his native Argentina. In a sense this work of translation foreshadowed the many collaborative works Borges would bring to fruition over the course of his career.

When the family moved to Europe in 1914, settling in Geneva, Switzerland, Borges's education in French commenced; though at first he struggled in the language, he eventually mastered it. His first article in French was published in the Geneva newspaper *La Feuille* in August 1919.

When the family moved to Spain, Borges came into contact with many poets and writers, most significantly with Rafael Cansinos-Assens, who had founded the ultraist literary movement. Borges wrote much about Cansinos and *ultraismo* in the several literary reviews in which he published while in

Simplicity became the keynote of the sort of ultraism Borges evolved with Argentine friends. He said they "came to the conclusion that Spanish ultraism was overburdened—after the manner of futurism—with modernity and gadgets. . . . What we wanted to write was essential poetry—poems beyond the here and now, free of local color and contemporary circumstances." Artist Carol Anthony presents blank tableaux in *Lipsos Room,* created in 1989.

Spain, and he took the ideas of the movement back to Argentina when he returned to Buenos Aires.

Upon his return to Argentina, Borges began his literary career, especially its collaborative aspect, in earnest. Under the tutelage of his new mentor, Macedonio Fernández, and in collaboration with a group of writers that included Borges's cousin Guillermo Juan Borges and Guillermo's cousin Norah Lange, Borges spread the message of ultraism through the group's literary review *Prisma* in 1921 and 1922. Publication of articles on the subject then followed in other reviews in Argentina as well as in Spain, and the group then formed another review called *Proa*. During this period Borges was also writing and publishing his first books of poetry and essays, *Fervor of Buenos Aires, Luna de enfrente, Inquisiciones,* and *El tamaño de mi esperanza.* He was also involved in a review called *La Prensa* and another called *Martín Fierro* (after the famous character in Argentine poetry).

In the 1930s Borges met some of the most influential thinkers and writers in Hispanic letters of the time. In 1930 the Mexican writer Alfonso Reyes arrived in Buenos Aires as ambassador after spending several years in Spain, and Borges was very much influenced by his prose style and his erudition. Likewise, the Dominican linguist and literary critic Pedro Henríquez Ureña came to Argentina seeking refuge from the Trujillo dictatorship. Henríquez would collaborate with Borges in the editing and publication of important literary reviews in Buenos Aires. Perhaps most significant of all, Borges met Adolfo Bioy Casares in 1931 in Argentina, and the two worked together closely, coauthoring works of fiction, especially in the detective genre, throughout their respective careers (Bioy Casares is renowned for his works of fiction, such as *La invención de Morel,* in and outside of Argentina). Another important collaborator was Victoria Ocampo, a significant figure in the groundbreaking literary review *Sur,* in which Borges published and labored.

A unique feature of Borges's collaborative works was the use of pseudonyms to conceal the identities of the coauthors. In the 1940s, together with Adolfo Bioy Casares but concealed behind the joint nom de plume Bustos Domecq, Borges coauthored several collections of stories. Other collections in 1967 and 1977 bore the same pseudonym, though the joke was by then known to all the readers of both Bioy Casares and Borges.

Borges also enjoyed many important collaborative efforts later in life, though more as mentor than as coauthor or protégé, especially with Norman Thomas di Giovanni, an American professor, and with María Kodama, who would later become Borges's wife, heir, and director of the foundation devoted to his estate and studies in Buenos Aires. Di Giovanni translated many of Borges's works into English, traveled with him, and also arranged for his visiting professorships in the United States until his last years.

SOURCES FOR FURTHER STUDY

Di Giovanni, Norman Thomas, ed. *In Memory of Borges.* London: Constable, 1988.

FICCIONES

Genre: Short story
Subgenre: Fantasy
Time period: Various
Published: Buenos Aires, 1944

Themes and Issues. *Ficciones* consists of the 8 short stories originally published in *The Garden of Forking Paths* (1941) and a second collection of 10 stories, *Artifices,* which were first printed as part of *Ficciones.* The book is widely regarded as Borges's most important work of fiction. Ranging from the discovery of a fictitious planet, Uqbar, in "Tlön, Uqbar, Orbis Tertius" to rewriting *Don Quixote* word for word in "Pierre Menard, Author of Don Quixote" to infallible and total recall in "Funes the Memorious," the stories are flights of fancy filled with references to historical events, people, books, and places, both imagined and real, without any distinction to alert the reader as to what is serious and what is tongue in cheek or merely fictional. Borges himself in the prologue employs the fiction that he is not the author of "The Library of Babel," a story that inspired *The Name of the Rose,* the novel by Umberto Eco. He also claims that "Death and the Compass" (which was first published in this collection) is a detective story, yet the clues to the murder parallel the tetragrammaton, the unutterable personal name of God in the Jewish tradition, and the story ends with the murderer, Scarlach, killing the detective and saying to him, "The next time I kill you, I promise you the labyrinth made of the single straight line which is invisible and everlasting," suggesting a cycli-

Borges said "The Library of Babel" was meant as "a nightmare version or magnification" of the library where he worked. It contains all possible combinations of his fictional world's alphabet, "that is, all that is able to be expressed, in every language. *All*—the detailed history of the future, the autobiographies of the archangels, the faithful catalog of the Library, thousands and thousands of false catalogs, the proof of the falsity of those false catalogs, a proof of the falsity of the *true* catalog . . . ." Alex Clark's *Inside the Tower of Babel* depicts the interior of the legendary tower.

cal repetition of history with ever-growing complexities.

Analysis. In *Ficciones,* Borges brings to bear all his powers of erudition and imagination in a way that took Latin American fiction out of the realm of the provincial and into a universe previously unseen. With his vast knowledge of languages, books, and places, Borges intermingles fact and fiction; he quotes authors real and imaginary in French, Latin, English, and Spanish; and he draws upon philosophical, historical, and religious traditions usually ignored or sidestepped by other writers. In "Tlön, Uqbar, Orbis Tertius," for example, he suggests the idea that the planet was only recently created and then peopled with beings with false memories of a past that never existed. In "The Circular Ruins" Borges plays with the idea that humans are merely the product of the dreams of another being, and in "The Garden of Forking Paths," he addresses the multiplicity of possible futures: "Time is forever dividing itself toward innumerable futures and in one of them I am your enemy." The stories abound with such references and allusions, so many that the effect is dizzying even to the most informed reader.

SOURCES FOR FURTHER STUDY

Balderston, Daniel. *The Literary Universe of Jorge Luis Borges. An Index to References and Allusions to Persons, Titles, and Places in His Writings.* Westport, CT: Greenwood Press, 1986.

Fishburn, Evelyn, and Psiche Hughes. *A Dictionary of Jorge Luis Borges.* London: Duckworth, 1990.

Irwin, John T. *The Mystery to a Solution: Poe, Borges, and the Analytic Detective Story.* Baltimore: Johns Hopkins University Press, 1994.

THE ALEPH

Genre: Short story
Subgenre: Fantasy
Time period: Various
Published: Buenos Aires, 1949

Themes and Issues. *The Aleph,* the book's title, refers to the first letter of the Hebrew alphabet and, in the story of the same name, to a theoretical point in space that provides a window through which to view all points in space; there is supposedly an aleph in the basement of a poet's house. After having viewed the entirety of the universe through the aleph, the narrator of the story finds everything and everyone he sees thereafter to be familiar to him, until finally forgetfulness returns, and he can begin to see the world as other mortals do, a mixture of the familiar and the unknown. In "The Other Death" Borges approaches the theme of history and revisionism through the story of Pedro Damián and two versions of his death. In "The Immortal" Borges addresses the blessings and curses of living forever by taking the reader on a journey to a river that makes men immortal; in the end it is the journey itself that constitutes immortality, and thereafter, the immortal man spends his years in search of a possible antidote to eternal life. Some of the stories of this collection were made into films: "Emma Zunz," the tale of a daughter avenging the humiliation suffered by her father; "The Dead Man," in which a man, envious of another's power and his woman, is murdered; and "The Story of the Warrior and the Captive Woman," which includes a tale from the Borges family history. These became film scripts in Spanish, and "The Intruder," the story of two brothers who share a kept woman but choose to kill her rather than break their fraternal bonds, was filmed in Portuguese. "Emma Zunz" also inspired a French film.

Analysis. With their emphasis on realism, most of the stories that have been mentioned above (as evidenced by the films they inspired) are more solidly in the mainstream of the short story genre than is typical for Borges, although most end with an unexpected plot twist. Borges is still fascinated, of course, with more metaphysical themes: immortality and death in "The Immortal"; religion and heresy and shared destinies in "The Theologians"; and a favorite theme, the labyrinth, in "The Two Kings and the Two Labyrinths" and "Abencaján el Bojarí, Dead in His Labyrinth." This theme

Borges's short story "The Aleph" combines literary comedy with the infinite. A would-be poet with no talent somehow lives above a mysterious place where the entire universe is captured in a single dot. The narrator takes a look: "The Aleph's diameter was probably little more than an inch, but all space was there. . . . I saw a silvery cobweb in the center of a black pyramid; I saw a splintered labyrinth (it was London); I saw, close up, unending eyes watching themselves in me as in a mirror . . . ." Michael Poulton's 1996 collage *The Shape of the Universe* reflects a similar infinite perspective.

had been contemplated in some of the stories of *Ficciones* as well: "The Garden of Forking Paths," "The Circular Ruins," "The Library of Babel," and "Death and the Compass."

SOURCES FOR FURTHER STUDY

Di Giovanni, Norman Thomas, ed. *The Borges Tradition.* London: Constable, in association with the Anglo-Argentine Society, 1995.

Hernández Martín, Jorge. *Readers and Labyrinths: Detective Fiction in Borges, Bustos Domecq and Eco.* New York: Garland, 1995.

Isbister, Rob, and Peter Standish. *A Concordance to the Works of Jorge Luis Borges (1899–1986), Argentine Author.* 7 vols. Lewiston, NY: Edwin Mellen Press, 1991.

DREAMTIGERS

Genre: Short story
Subgenres: Various
Published: Buenos Aires, 1960

Themes and Issues. The name of this anthology of short prose pieces, essays, and poems selected by Borges, *Dreamtigers,* is a translation of the title of the second piece of the collection rather than a literal translation of the title of the first story, "El hacedor" ("The Maker"), which is also the Spanish title of the whole collection. This first story seems to refer to Borges himself; as the protagonist slowly goes blind, the world recedes around him, and in its place comes a universe of memories. Likewise, the piece entitled "Dreamtigers" refers to Borges's fascination with tigers as a child. In "The Veiled Mirrors" there is an apparently autobiographical reference to a woman Borges met who went insane and saw his image in mirrors, as though he were pursuing her, rather than her own face looking back. Very few of the prose pieces of *Dreamtigers* could be called short stories in the strict sense. Borges describes some of the pieces as parables and others as dialogues; "prose poems" would also be an apt description for many of these very brief narratives. The references and allusions that Borges employed in his short stories, the names of places, people, and books, whether real or imagined, are in this collection more often connected to his own life, to the history of his family or that of Argentina, or even to recent events around him. Some of the poems are titled "Allusions" and refer to moments of family and Argentinian history. Borges states in the epilogue, "Of all the books I have delivered to the printing press, none, I believe, is as personal as this collected and disorganized 'silva of varied reading,' precisely because it abounds in reflections and in interpolations."

Analysis. Published in 1960, *Dreamtigers* represents the work of Borges the mature poet and author. The political intrigues of the 1930s and 1940s are well behind him, his work has gained recognition throughout the world, and blindness has come in full, as has acceptance of that blindness. The themes of these stories are

From "Veiled Mirrors," one of the stories in Borges's 1960 collection, *Dreamtigers:* "One of my insistent pleas to God and my guardian angel was that I not dream of mirrors. . . . I feared sometimes that they would begin to veer off from reality; other times, that I would see my face in them disfigured by strange misfortunes." Here we see Robert Stivers's 2002 artwork *Series 8: Face in Mirror,* in which a somewhat tentative figure, much like Borges's character, avoids a direct glance in the mirror.

SOME INSPIRATIONS BEHIND BORGES'S WORK

Jorge Luis Borges's parents were Anglophiles and avid readers with a sizable collection of books, especially works of English and American literature. As a result, young Georgie, as he was called, was surrounded by the English language and literature from infancy. The first novel he read was Mark Twain's *Huckleberry Finn.* Even famous works of Spanish literature, such as Miguel Cervantes's *Don Quixote,* were first read by the young Borges in English translation. The stories of Edgar Allan Poe, the tales of *The Thousand and One Nights,* the works of Jules Verne and H. G. Wells: these were all favorites of Borges, and their influence on his own stories was evident and significant. At age 10 he published his first piece of writing, a translation into Spanish of Oscar Wilde's "The Happy Prince."

When the family moved to Geneva, Switzerland, Borges's focus turned next to the French language and literature, French being the language of instruction at his school. Here Borges encountered the works of Guy de Maupassant, Victor Hugo, Gustave Flaubert, and other giants of French literature. As his studies progressed, Borges learned to read German on his own and read *Der Golem* by Gustav Meyrink. The figure of the golem became an important theme in Borges's later writings.

Having mastered German, Borges came into contact (in his typically unconventional style) with a work of poetry whose influence would be very important in the young man's life: Walt Whitman's *Leaves of Grass,* in the German translation. He later ordered an edition in English and read it constantly.

His mastery of the German language would also lead Borges to Franz Kafka, whose short fiction proved an influence on the stories that Borges himself would write, especially those in *The Garden of Forking Paths, Ficciones, The Aleph,* and *Death and the Compass.*

Upon the family's relocation to Spain, Borges associated with several poets and had his first works published, an article written in French and then a poem, "Himno del mar" (Hymn of the sea), in Spanish. His meetings with Spanish writers led to his association with the ultraist movement in literature, which called for a complete renovation of Spanish letters. *Ultraismo* was an idea Borges would take back to Buenos Aires.

Back in Argentina, it was the unfortunate accident, in 1938, in which Borges fell in a stairway that turned him to fiction. The experience inspired the short story "The South," and many of the other stories that followed owed something of their hallucinatory feeling to this accident.

The hallucinations Borges suffered after his head injury made him fear for his mind. Listening to his mother read aloud *Out of the Silent Planet*, C. S. Lewis's surreal novel about life on Mars, Borges began to cry. "My mother asked me why the tears. 'I'm crying because I understand,' I said." His fear drove him to write his first story; better that than fail at something he had already done and know it was all over for him. The 1983 collage artwork above (artist unknown), a phantasmagoria in itself, is entitled *Young People In Particular Will Find It.*

naturally more personal and more reflective, less fanciful than his previous works. Perhaps most indicative of this movement toward the personal is the short piece "Borges and I," in which the author refers to himself in the third person and to an unknown "I" in the first person, presumably himself as well. "Things happen to him, the other one, to Borges," he begins, and then he enumerates differences between himself and Borges the author, who will endure through his written words, while the "I" slowly slips into oblivion. The piece ends with this disheartening exclamation: "Thus is my life a flight, and I lose everything, and everything belongs to oblivion, or to him. I don't know which one of the two of us is writing this page." Perhaps the aging writer is finally contemplating his own mortality.

SOURCES FOR FURTHER STUDY

Alazraki, Jaime. *Jorge Luis Borges.* New York: Columbia University Press, 1971.

Molloy, Sylvia. *Signs of Borges.* Durham, NC: Duke University Press, 1994.

Sturrock, John. *Paper Tigers: The Ideal Fictions of Jorge Luis Borges.* New York: Oxford University Press, 1978.

A PERSONAL ANTHOLOGY

Genres: Essays, poems, and short stories
Subgenres: Various styles and genres
Time period: Various
Published: Buenos Aires, 1961

Themes and Issues. *A Personal Anthology* does not include new or previously unpublished work of Borges. Its themes and content, however, represent a repetition or even a reaffirmation of his preoccupation with identity, history, and (according to Anthony Kerrigan, the author of the translation's foreword) "a compulsive instinct." This instinct leads Borges to affirm, as Kerrigan again puts it, that "if in the universe—in the entire history of the universe even—there is or has ever been anyone who could be a duplicate of himself, then the meaning of all life, all lives, is altogether suspect." Borges admits that his "preferences have dictated this book" and that "sympathies and differences," rather than chronological order, were the guiding forces in the selection and organization of the included pieces, which include essays (such as "A New Refutation of Time" and "Forms of a Legend"), poetry, and short fiction.

Analysis. In common with the rest of Borges's work, *A Personal Anthology* is notable for inventiveness, erudition, and the use of fantastical elements. Its mix of poetry, essay, and short story gives the most complete overview of the writer's work available in a single short volume. The juxtaposition of works on metaphysical topics, such as the poem "The Cyclical Night," with others on cultural themes, such as the poem "The Tango," and with still others on philosophy, such as the essay "A New Refutation of Time," reveals a full-length portrait of Borges the author.

SOURCES FOR FURTHER STUDY

Dunham, Lowell, and Ivar Ivask. *The Cardinal Points of Borges.* Norman: University of Oklahoma Press, 1971.

Merrell, Floyd. *Unthinking Thinking: Jorge Luis Borges, Mathematics and the New Physics.* West Lafayette, IN: Purdue University Press, 1991.

Sarlo, Beatriz. *Jorge Luis Borges: The Writer on the Edge.* London: Verso, 1993.

Other Works

"THREE VERSIONS OF JUDAS" (1944). In "Three Versions of Judas," drawn from the collection *Ficciones,* a religious scholar, Nils Runeberg, argues that Judas is not the traitor he is portrayed to be in the Gospels; rather, it is Judas himself that is the Christ. Judas's betrayal, to identify the Messiah to the Roman soldiers and Jewish authorities, was unnecessary, as Jesus was known to all by virtue of his teaching in public. Likewise, it was Judas's death and not the crucifixion of Jesus that was actually the redeeming act of sacrifice necessary to reveal the divinity of the Lord. Runeberg dies of an aneurysm in 1912, driven mad by the implications of his own arguments yet hoping to suffer in hell with the Redeemer.

"THE BABYLON LOTTERY" (1944). "The Babylon Lottery" is also collected in *Ficciones*. It describes how a simple lottery, played every 70 nights in the labyrinths of the gods, is gradually transformed from a game of pure chance into a representation of the order, or chaos, of the universe. In their original form, the narrator says, the drawings "did not appeal to all the faculties of men: only to their hope." To attract a following, the merchants add a number of adverse lots to the drawings; a fine or punishment is imposed on the ticket's bearer when the adverse lot is drawn. This element of danger piques the interest of the players, and the lottery becomes very successful. When a slave steals a ticket and the punishment fixed by the law for theft coincides with the penalty prescribed by the lottery for that adverse lot, the game and the company that operates it become all-powerful until Babylon itself is "nothing but an infinite game of chance."

"DEUTSCHES REQUIEM" (1949). "Deutsches Requiem" is one of the stories in *The Aleph*. (The title, which means "German Requiem," was taken from the name of the celebrated choral work by Johannes Brahms.) Before his execution for the war crimes of torture and murder, Otto Dietrich zur Linde describes his participation in the war, his transformation into the subdirector of the concentration camp at Tarnowitz, his reflections on the parallels between this transformation and the one Germany must experience to bring in the new order, and his studies in the philosophy of Nietzsche, Spengler, and Schopenhauer and how these metaphysical concepts influenced his acceptance of Nazism. Borges, in the epilogue to *The Aleph*, states, "In the last

war no one could have felt more strongly than I that Germany be defeated; no one could have felt more than I the tragedy of the German fate; 'Deutsches Requiem' wants to understand this fate."

"DIALOGUE OF THE DEAD" (1960). In "Dialogue of the Dead," from *Dreamtigers*, two dead men, Rosas and Quiroga, hold a conversation in the afterlife in which they discuss their separate but intertwined destinies. Rosas is confronted by Quiroga and others, presumably his enemies, as he arrives. Quiroga claims that he will be remembered for the manner of his death, which he owes to Rosas, while Rosas fled from a warrior's death out of fear. Quiroga further explains that he is "going to be erased, to get another face and another destiny, because history is filled with violent men. I don't know who the other will be, what they will do with me, but I know he will not have fear." Rosas answers: "It may be that I wasn't made to be dead, but these places and this discussion seem like a dream to me, and not a dream dreamt by me, but by another, who is yet to be born." This theme of cyclical repetition occurs in many other Borges pieces, as does the idea of men being characters in the dreams of another being.

"AVERROËS' SEARCH" (1949). "Averroës' Search," too, is part of *The Aleph*. An Islamic scholar, whose lengthy Arabic name is eventually shortened to Averroës, is studying the *Rhetoric* and *Poetics* of Aristotle. Averroës is confounded by the meaning of the words *tragedy* and *comedy* as used by Aristotle. After conversations with a traveler, Abulcasím, in the house of a mutual friend, Farach, Averroës suddenly comes to understand the meaning he is searching for, and at that instant he disappears from sight, along with his home, possessions, slaves, and friends "and perhaps even the Guadalquivir." The nameless narrator explains that he, too, like Averroës, is searching for understanding, and when the scholar Averroës achieves the goal of enlightenment, he ceases to exist in the mind of the narrator.

In Borges's short story "Averroës' Search" the character and his fictional world disappear, leaving the narrator to explain: "I sensed that Averroës, striving to imagine a drama without ever having suspected what a theater was, was no more absurd than I, who strove to imagine Averroës with no material other than some fragments from Renan, Lane, and Asín Palacios. I sensed, on the last page, that my narrative was a symbol of the man I was while I wrote it, and that to write that story I had to be that man, and that to be that man I had to write that story, and so to infinity. (The instant I stop believing in him, Averroës disappears.)"—somewhat like the figure in Alfredo Castañeda's 1999 painting *Our Waiting,* only this time into the horizon.

"MARTÍN FIERRO" (1960). Also from *Dreamtigers,* "Martín Fierro" takes its name from the title of one of Argentina's most famous works of literature. It is the tale of the archetypal gaucho of the Argentine pampas. Borges's work enumerates several historical events: the battles at Ituzaingó and Ayacucho and a massacre of unitarian forces by republican tyrants. These are representative of the things and places that inspire works of literature and of art. In each of these references, Borges pronounces, "These things are as if they had never been." By contrast, the work *Martín Fierro* will endure, even though it is only a dream experienced in a hotel room sometime around 1860. "This that once was will be again, infinitely," he states. He goes on to say in the final phrase of the piece, "the dream of one is part of the memory of all."

Most manuscripts of Borges's works are held in private collections. Some have been lent for exhibitions at museums. The Fundación Jorge Luis Borges, in Buenos Aires, holds the personal library, the photographs, and some personal effects of the author. This foundation was established by María Kodama, who was the sole heir of Borges. (Another foundation, the Fundación San Telmo, is described below.)

Aarhus University. This university, situated in Denmark, has a Borges studies program. The program's Web site has pages in English, Spanish, and French, and it includes bibliographies and on-line study sites (www. hum.au.dk/romansk/borges).

Complete Works. Three attempts have been made to publish the *obras completas* (complete works) of Borges in Spanish. The first publication was undertaken in 1974 by the Spanish firm Ultramar; it included everything Borges published between 1923 and 1972. In 1981 there was a complete edition of the collaborative works published by Lectorum Publications of New Jersey. In 1989 the publisher Emecâe (Buenos Aires) released the most complete of all the "complete" editions. Sad to say, none have ever been made available in English translation.

Documentaries. At least seven significant documentary films about Borges, two of which are in English, have been released since the mid-1960s. The English-language ones are *The Inner World of Jorge Luis Borges* (1969; directed by Harold Mantell; United States) and *Borges and I* (1983; David Wheatley; United Kingdom). Of the remainder one is in French, the others are in Spanish: *Borges* (1966; Luis Angel Bellalba; Argentina), *Borges* (1969; André Camp and José María Berzosa; France), *Borges sobre Borges* (1975; Carlos Gdansky and Adolfo García Videla; Argentina), *Borges para millones* (1978; Ricardo Wulicher and Bernardo Kamin; Argentina), and *Los paseos de Borges* (1980; Adolfo García Videla; Argentina).

Fundación San Telmo. Like the Fundación Jorge Luis Borges, the Fundación San Telmo is situated in Buenos Aires. It maintains a Web site with photos and bibliographies and offers Borges's works and related materials for purchase. Its pages are available only in Spanish. It is easy to navigate, but it does have a certain commercial focus, which is presumably intended to raise funds for the foundation's work and maintenance. Of particular note is the fact that the San Telmo collection holds Borges's magnificent letters to Estela Canto, with whom he had been deeply in love (www.fst.com.ar).

The Modern Word. The many fascinating articles on dozens of writers active during the past century make this literary Web site a must-see for lovers of good modern literature. Among its many other riches, the site contains a thorough bibliography of the works available in English on Borges. It also includes access to photos, sound recordings, and scholarly papers published on the Web (www. themodernword.com/borges).

TODD W. BURRELL

Bertolt Brecht

BORN: February 10, 1898, Augsburg, Bavaria (Germany)

DIED: August 14, 1956, East Berlin

IDENTIFICATION: German playwright, poet, and short-story writer best known for a group of politically committed dramas and for his work with the composer Kurt Weill.

SIGNIFICANCE: Bertolt Brecht wished to encourage social and political change through his writing. To promote his ideas, he developed what he called an "epic theater." This type of theater aimed at doing more than entertain. It attempted to arouse theatergoers to act against injustice. In *The Threepenny Opera* (1929) the main characters—thieves and beggars—ape the middle-class pursuit of material wealth. Greed, Brecht seems to say, has made them the outcasts they are. Brecht used the existing techniques of the stage and created new ones to hammer home his points. His politically pointed plays, together with his theories of drama, influenced the shape and development of the theater.

The Writer's Life

Eugen Berthold Friedrich Brecht was born on February 10, 1898, in Augsburg, a medieval town in the southern German state of Bavaria. (The spelling Bertolt came later.) His father, an influential town citizen, also named Berthold, managed the Haindl paper mill. The family, which included a younger son, Walther, enjoyed a moderately well-to-do middle-class existence. A friend of the Brechts described Brecht senior as strict and crotchety. Though it would later become fashionable in German literature to criticize one's father, Brecht never did so.

The ever charismatic Bertolt Brecht around 1950. Meeting Brecht, said the writer Elias Canetti, he felt like an object being sized up by a pawnbroker as worthless. A theater colleague said Brecht swept away resistance in his listeners, "amiably advising them not to squander time—just to capitulate." Behind his charm, though, the singer Lotte Lenya said that Brecht was "forever assessing people for what they could contribute to him (and inevitably getting it)."

An Early Literary Influence. Brecht's Protestant mother, Sophie Brezing, kept a Lutheran Bible at home. Reading it affected the future author. Though his plays, poems, and stories often criticize religion (Brecht's father was a Catholic), they frequently contain biblical references. One source for his play *The Caucasian Chalk Circle (Der kaukasische Kreidekreis),* produced and published in 1948, is the Old Testament story of the Judgment of Solomon. His short story "Before the Flood" ("Vor der Sintflut," 1925) concerns Noah's ark. Brecht said early in his career that of all the books he read, the Bible had the greatest impact on him (he had, as a youth, read very widely).

School and Afterward. Though apparently bored with most aspects of elementary and high school life, Brecht appeared to enjoy Latin and composition. In 1914, when he was 16, several of his poems appeared in a local newspaper. They were signed Berthold Eugen. By the second year of World War I, Brecht, now 18 years old, was nearly expelled from high school for writing an essay questioning German patriotism. He succeeded in graduating and in 1917 enrolled at the University of Munich to study medicine. Soon after, he was drafted into military service. As a hospital orderly he witnessed the tragedy of war. His well-known poem "The Legend of the Dead Soldier" ("Die Legende vom toten Soldaten") comes from this experience. The antiwar poem resulted in his being placed on the "enemies list" of the growing National Socialist (Nazi) Party.

The Developing Artist. Brecht returned to Munich after his hospital duty in Augsburg. In addition to studying at the university again, he wrote poetry and plays and performed his music in public. Accompanying himself on the guitar, he sang his lyrics in taverns and coffee houses. A photograph taken between 1919 and 1920 shows Brecht on a cabaret stage playing a clarinet, cap slung low over one eye. His interest in music, literature, and the cynical lyrics performed in cabaret skits was gradually finding voice in his work.

Brecht's Personal Appeal.

Shy and quiet, though eager to speak when excited about matters, Brecht in late adolescence and young manhood often struck others as destined for success. In the early 1920s, perhaps trying to look like a tough character from one of his future plays, the tall, thin playwright wore "that eternal cap," a pair of cheap, steel-rimmed glasses, and a shabby leather jacket, one friend recalled. In Munich the older novelist Lion Feuchtwanger befriended Brecht and helped him to get established as a writer.

Uncertain Future.

Like most other authors, Brecht was eager to succeed, to conquer the big city and become famous. However, after several attempts to remain in Berlin, a vibrant, exciting European city in the 1920s, he returned to Munich penniless. There he wrote drama reviews for a socialist paper. In the spring of 1922, in Berlin again, worn down and undernourished, he was admitted to Charité Hospital to regain his strength. Despite the difficulties he encountered, the time in Berlin proved useful to Brecht. When his play *Drums in the Night* (*Trommeln in der Nacht*) opened in September 1922, several drama critics he had met in Berlin traveled to Munich to review his work for German newspapers. The play, which in-

Grosstadt, or *Metropolis,* by artist George Grosz captures the exuberance and ugliness of Berlin. Note the American flag in the upper left: jazz was the fashion, and Brecht set *Mahagonny* and other works in a fractured version of the United States. "Is here no telephone?" goes a typical scrap of English stranded in *Mahagonny*'s dialogue.

cluded a song version of "The Legend of the Dead Soldier," won an important award and was published that year. At age 24 Bertolt Brecht was becoming someone to reckon with in German theater.

Domestic Life.

In 1919 Brecht had fallen in love with the singer Marianne Zoff. Before they wed in 1922, they had a son, Frank. Soon after the marriage, a daughter, Hanne, was born. During the marriage the playwright saw his first book of poems published and four of his plays produced for the first time. He wrote one of them with Feuchtwanger. Five years later the marriage to Marianne Zoff ended. By now another child had been born, a daughter, Barbara, to the actress Helene Weigel, whom Brecht married in 1929. He remained with Helene Weigel the rest of his life.

Political Awakening. Sometime in 1926 Brecht began reading and attending lectures on the German political philosopher and socialist Karl Marx. Marx's ideas form the basis of communism. As Brecht embraced the beliefs of the Communist Party, his plays took on more pronounced Marxist themes. Brecht had also begun conceiving a type of play that would startle audiences. Where German life and culture had grown stagnant, the plays he planned were to awaken people from their self-satisfied lives. Brecht succeeded with *The Threepenny Opera*, produced in 1928. Its jazzy music by Kurt Weill, its unusual staging, its criticism of middle-class life, and the way it captured the chaos of European life after World War I made the play an immediate success. Soon it was performed across Europe. Twenty-six years later it enjoyed a history-making off-Broadway run in New York City.

A year earlier Brecht and Weill had collaborated on a short "song play." The now successful playwright lengthened the short piece into *The Rise and Fall of the City of Mahagonny*, published in 1929 in Berlin as *Aufstieg und Fall der Stadt Mahagonny*. Its innovative staging and the chaos of the final scene (the city burns as actors sing about money) caused a scandal at the play's premiere in Leipzig, Germany. This play and *The Threepenny Opera* reflect the theme of much of Brecht's work—that human beings cannot be made perfect and that the continuous pursuit of money adds to their corruption. Political, social, and religious institutions further the corruption.

Flight from Home. Fearing the Nazis, in 1933 Brecht and his family fled Germany. They lived as exiles for 15 years—in Denmark, Sweden, Finland, and Switzerland. Brecht

Berlin, the Lustgarten, in February 1934. In 1923 Brecht was rehearsing *Edward II* in Nazi-ridden Munich when Hitler's men tried to take over the city. He considered them "sad little curs," but in the early days he could enjoy Hitler's gift for mass spectacle. "He has the advantages of a man who's done all his theatergoing in the upper circle," the playwright once said. Eleven years later Brecht had fled and the new regime was reshaping the nation.

HIGHLIGHTS IN BRECHT'S LIFE

1898	Bertolt Brecht is born on February 10 in Augsburg, Bavaria, Germany.
1917	Graduates from high school; enters the University of Munich.
1919	Writes plays in Munich; is befriended by novelist Lion Feuchtwanger.
1922	Wins important drama prize; marries Marianne Zoff, who bears him two children, Frank and Hanne.
1924	Moves to Berlin; becomes assistant to the theatrical producer Max Reinhardt.
1926–1927	Develops interest in Marxism; divorces Marianne Zoff; publishes book of poems.
1928	*The Threepenny Opera* opens to instant acclaim.
1929	Brecht marries Helene Weigel, with whom he has two children, Barbara and Stefan.
1933	Leaves Germany with his family to settle on an island off Denmark.
1935	Travels to the Soviet Union to plan anti-Nazi speeches to broadcast over Moscow radio and the British Broadcasting Corporation; is officially deprived of German citizenship by the Nazis.
1939–1940	Leaves Denmark for Sweden; moves to Helsinki, Finland, after the Nazi invasion of Denmark and Norway.
1942	Works in Hollywood with the filmmaker Fritz Lang.
1945	Collaborates on a translation of *Galileo* with the actor Charles Laughton.
1948	Returns to Germany; founds Berliner Ensemble.
1956	Dies in East Berlin on August 14 and is buried there.

wrote some of his best plays during this period, among them *Mother Courage and Her Children (Mutter Courage und ihre Kinder)*. The play was first published in 1941 in New York, not in German but in English, and in the same year was produced in Zurich, Switzerland.

The playwright's exile took him to America, too. From 1941 to 1947, Brecht lived in a small home near Hollywood in Santa Monica, California. He collaborated with the German director Fritz Lang on the movie *Hangmen Also Die* (1943). With the actor Charles Laughton

A Czech professor, played by Walter Brennan, faces his interrogator in Brecht's screenplay, *Hangmen Also Die.* The 1943 United Artists film was Brecht's closest brush with big-time moviemaking during his six years in Hollywood. Fritz Lang, the creator of the motion pictures *Metropolis* and *M,* directed. Brecht's name didn't show up on the final script, and he didn't get far with the angle he wanted: that the mass was more important than the individual, with the Czech people resisting the Nazis more effectively than the resistance leaders did. A secretary at United Artists came up with the title in a contest; Brecht wanted "Trust the People."

he wrote a translation of his play *The Life of Galileo (Leben des Galilei),* which, like *Mother Courage,* was produced in Zurich (1943). It was published in 1956 in Berlin. Though he had been safe from the war and had an extended stay in New York as well as living in California, Brecht never embraced American life and culture the way he did that of other countries where he had lived and traveled.

Exile's Return. In 1948 Brecht returned to Berlin, a city now sharply divided into the democratic western and the communist eastern sectors. The cold war had begun. Still, Brecht was home in Germany, and the communist government was subsidizing his writing at the Theater am Schiffbauerdamm. The acting company Brecht founded, the famous Berliner Ensemble, produced his and others' works in East Berlin and elsewhere.

Brecht's Final Years. The playwright, despite increasingly failing health, remained lively and alert up to the end of his life. He died on August 14, 1956, of heart trouble, a coronary thrombosis. His tombstone in the cemetery near his Berlin home has only two words on it: BERTOLT BRECHT.

The Writer's Work

Although a dramatist, Bertolt Brecht also wrote poems, short stories, political commentaries, and important notes and essays on the theater. His plays are known for their satirical songs and dialogue, for their nonrealistic staging, and for their attempts at political instruction. To describe the purpose of his work, he used the German word *Lehrstücke,* which means "instruction" or "teaching pieces." With his teaching he would attempt to change the same middle class he grew up in and came to dislike. In his view the German middle class would follow anyone in power, even Adolf Hitler, if the person served its interests. The middle class cared nothing for less fortunate people. As a budding playwright he added a hatred of war and a distrust of post–World War I German politics to his dislike of the bourgeoisie, the middle class. He wanted to teach audiences to change the Europe (even the world) of the future. The theater itself needed changing if it was to be a place of instruction.

Epic Theater. Brecht called the type of theater he would develop "epic." It differed significantly from the traditional theater, which he considered no longer useful to the modern age. The setting of a drama written for epic theater

The German 1920s live on in the America of 1946. Brecht watches while George Grosz explains his art to actor Charles Laughton, who would stage Brecht's *Galileo* on Broadway in 1947. Oddly, considering the picture they're looking at, Brecht admired Laughton's appetite and even produced an ode to his stomach. While most fat men carried theirs like plunder to be hidden, Brecht wrote, "the great Laughton recited his like a poem."

could change rapidly from country to country. One scene might be lengthy, the next brief. Scenes were often disconnected in time and place. Brecht provided directors with specific rules on how to direct plays. He instructed actors how to act and sing and musicians how to play the jazz music he incorporated in his work. Music and lyrics, often written by Kurt Weill, reinforced the play's political position. Actors, not trained vocalists, were cast in singing roles—actors would be able to distance themselves from a melody in a way musicians would not. "There is a kind of speaking-against-the-music which can have strong effects," he wrote. Such speaking-singing "is independent of music and rhythm."

Moreover, in his attempt to keep audiences from becoming too involved with the events portrayed onstage, Brecht intended to make those events seem strange to them. This ploy would prompt audiences to think about what they were watching. The safe emotional distance they maintained in the traditional theater would no longer be allowed. Accordingly, Brecht set his plays in distant locations often during earlier historical periods. *Galileo* takes place in seventeenth-century Italy, far away in time and place from wartime Germany. *St. Joan of the Stockyards (Die heilige Johanna der Schlachthöfe),* published in 1932 in Berlin though not produced until 1959 in Hamburg, is set in Chicago. Brecht hoped German the-

In 1945 the Red Army plants the Soviet flag atop Berlin's Brandenburg Gate; eastern Germany would stay under Soviet rule for 44 years. In 1947, Brecht testified before Congress about Communist activities—the chairman thanked him for setting a "good example"—and then fled the United States. Settling in East Germany, he received a chauffeured car and a fourteen-room villa. When the Soviets shot down German strikers in 1953, Brecht said the workers had been misled by "fascist elements" and he praised the "swift and accurate intervention of Soviet troops."

The youthful Brecht found inspiration reading the Bible or reading about ancient Rome. Though a non-Catholic, he had a lifelong fascination with St. Joan of Arc. Reflections of the saint's courage are seen in some of his plays, *St. Joan of the Stockyards,* for example. He was interested in and inspired by boxing, too. He thought a theater stage should resemble a boxing ring with the audience yelling and smoking at ringside. His work with various Munich cabaret performers and writers influenced him as well. Reading the work of Karl Marx probably changed Brecht more than anything, though. Marx provided a philosophical basis for Brecht's plays. So, too, did Brecht find the work of more established experimental playwrights inspiring. One of them, Erwin Piscator, had been trying different approaches to staging while Brecht was in Berlin in the 1920s. Piscator used treadmills, giant caricature drawings, and other devices on his stage. Though borrowing ideas from Piscator and other sources, Brecht made his own art unique and important. He went far beyond what other artists had accomplished.

atergoers would ask themselves, How would I act if I lived in that distant place or in that earlier time? Would I have tried to change the injustices seen onstage?

In epic theater, stagecraft, too, differed from that in the traditional theater. Stage lights were kept in full view of the audience, with no attempt to hide them. Still pictures, even films, appeared on screens above the stage. These visual devices provided the playwright another way to comment on the action. Such innovative techniques for using the physical space of the theater influenced the direction of modern drama.

People in Brecht's Plays. Brecht's characters struggle against political, economic, religious, and social forces. In the process they are often crushed. Sometimes his characters adopt the methods or beliefs of the systems or organizations opposing them. In *The Good Person of Setzuan (Der gute Mensch von Sezuan),* published in 1948 but first produced in 1943, Shen Te disguises herself as a stern male cousin so as not to lose her tobacco business. Shen Te's alter ego, the cousin, can better deal with the cruel people taking advantage of her. Other Brecht characters try to help oppressed people. In *St. Joan of the Stockyards,* Johanna Dark inspires striking workers but dies in the end. In *The Caucasian Chalk Circle,* Grusha Vashnadze, a kitchen maid, cares for an abandoned baby. These are three of Brecht's "better," more moral characters. They represent the playwright at his most optimistic. Generally, though, his characters are like Mackie the Knife, the small-time hoodlum in *Threepenny Opera,* or Pierpont Mauler, the meat-packing king in *St. Joan,* or Mrs. Begbick, the crime boss in *Mahagonny.* These characters use any means, legal or not, to get ahead in a vicious world run by big corporations, politicians, and religious authorities.

Artistic Legacy. Bertolt Brecht taught readers and playgoers that the theater can be larger—can mean more—than was ever deemed possible. Until the 1950s, however, his plays went largely unnoticed by American theatrical producers and American publishers. A New York production of *The Threepenny Opera* had failed in 1933. In 1940 only a translation

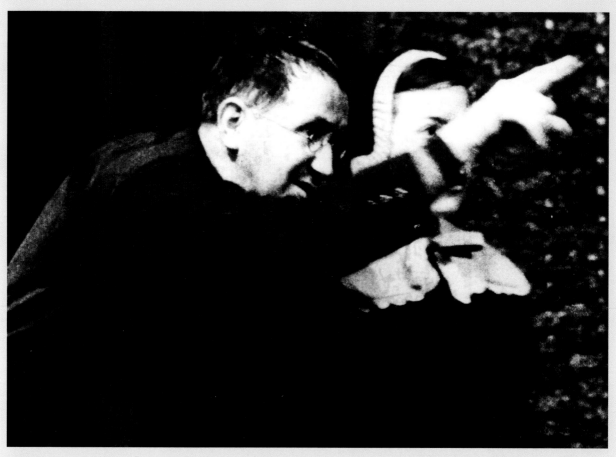

Brecht during rehearsals at the Berliner Ensemble. From 1949 until his death, he reigned over the troupe with his wife, the actress Helene Weigel. As a director, he wanted actors' movements to be few but telling, and he stressed the idea of a play as an argument that would drive the audience to choose a side. At the Ensemble directors had the last word, something Brecht once had to get through charm or temper tantrums. "Brecht was impossible and behaved vilely throughout," recalled John Houseman, *Galileo*'s producer. "But I have to admit he was dead right most of the time."

of Brecht's one novel was available in the United States. During the next 10 years, a mere three plays were published here, two by the University of Minnesota Press. The Brecht scholar Eric Bentley notes that "in the fifties Brecht caught on." This recognition was partly due to the success of the 1954 off-Broadway production of *The Threepenny Opera*. Since then Brecht's plays have been performed as regularly in the United States and other English-speaking countries as they had been performed for years in Europe and elsewhere. Brecht is now one of the most widely performed playwrights in the world. He made his political views entertaining, even moving, and his satiric language poetic. His characters, moreover, are remarkable for their richness. Together with his ideas for staging plays, these qualities make Brecht a major world dramatist.

BIBLIOGRAPHY

Bartram, Graham, and Anthony Waine, eds. *Brecht in Perspective.* New York: Longman, 1982.

Bentley, Eric. *The Brecht Commentaries: 1943–1980.* New York: Grove Press, 1981.

Cook, Bruce. *Brecht in Exile.* New York: Holt, 1982.

Fuegi, John. *Brecht and Company: Sex, Politics, and the Making of Modern Drama.* New York: Grove Press, 1994.

Hayman, Ronald. *Brecht: A Biography.* New York: Oxford University Press, 1983.

Hill, Claude. *Bertolt Brecht.* New York: Twayne, 1975.

Kleber, Pia, and Colin Visser, eds. *Reinterpreting Brecht: His Influence on Contemporary Drama and Film.* Cambridge: Cambridge University Press, 1990.

Mews, Siegfried. *A Bertolt Brecht Reference Companion.* Westport, CT: Greenwood Press, 1977.

Willett, John. *The Theater of Bertolt Brecht: A Study from Eight Aspects.* New York: New Directions, 1968.

THE THREEPENNY OPERA

Genre: Ballad opera
Subgenre: Satirical tragicomedy
Published: Berlin, 1929
Time period: Victorian England, late 1800s
Setting: London

Themes and Issues. Brecht distrusted capitalism. In such an economic system, either private owners or corporations control the prices, production, and distribution of goods. The economically and politically influential middle class often supported capitalism. In *The Threepenny Opera,* which is based on John Gay's *The Beggar's Opera* (1728), Brecht assigns middle-class values to thieves, beggars, and whores. Portions of the play are sung to scathing lyrics. When they saw *The Threepenny Opera,* Brecht hoped middle-class theatergoers would recognize their less attractive side, mainly their greed. Thus awakened, they might be more concerned with the plight of those who are exploited by capitalist enterprises.

The Plot. As the play begins, a ballad singer celebrates the adventures of a small-time crook, Mackie the Knife. Mr. Peachum, a more "respectable" businessman than Mackie, rents out beggars' outfits. For a price thieves choose from "five basic types of misery best adapted to touching the human heart." Once dressed in a basic type, they may opt to carry a sign that reads Shut Not Your Ears to Misery, or else It Is More Blessed to Give Than to Receive.

Mr. Peachum's honor is compromised when his daughter, Polly, runs off with Mackie. Peachum thinks Mackie the Knife can hardly measure up pro-

fessionally or morally to him. As Mackie's employees Robert the Saw, Wally the Weeper, and others decorate a stable with furniture stolen for Polly's wedding, in another area of town, Mr. and Mrs. Peachum agree to reward the whores Mackie frequently visits if they will turn him over to the police.

The subject of Christopher Pugliese's 2001 artwork *Greed* unabashedly highlights what Brecht may well have considered the fundamental evil of human nature. An insatiable desire for wealth and gain is the driving theme in Brecht's wildly successful play *The Threepenny Opera.* Opening off-Broadway in 1954, it ran for almost seven years. The Brecht-Weill collaboration had already seen 18 translations and some 10,000 performances a few years after it first appeared in 1928. The French writer Jean-Paul Sartre loved the songs, providing possibly the only link between him and Bobby Darin, who had a hit with "The Ballad of Mack the Knife" some 25 years later. Brecht wrote the ballad's lyrics, but who wrote the rest of the show has been disputed. Among other things, Brecht had to settle out of court for lifting German translations of poems by François de Villon. That trimmed his 62.5 percent share of the royalties to 60 percent.

Sentenced to be hanged at six o'clock on the morning of the queen's coronation, Mackie the Knife bribes Smith, an officer, and Tiger Brown, the police chief and Mackie's childhood friend, to free him. Polly, her parents, and others visit Mackie's jail cell. Unfortunately, Money Matthew and Hook-finger Jacob have not gotten to the bank to withdraw the bribe money because of the crowded streets on Coronation Day. As Mackie is about to be hanged, in gallops a mounted messenger. By order of the queen, Mackie is to be released and made a nobleman with a castle and a generous pension. Thus, Brecht meets middle-class playgoers' all-too-common expectations for a happy ending and ridicules them at the same time.

Analysis. Brecht sets the play in England. He hoped doing so would distance German audiences from thinking of their country and thus better enable him to communicate his message. To further distance playgoers from associating too closely with the onstage action, at key places Brecht has lighted signboards lowered from above. He once wrote that "lowering the caption title on the boards" undercuts the surprise element a song or other action might have and thus forces actors to make songs "striking by entirely different means." Yet another sign might give audiences permission to smoke. Brecht employed these stage devices to alert all Peachums and Mackies in the real world to be aware of their moral weaknesses regarding money.

SOURCES FOR FURTHER STUDY

Dharwadker, Aparna. "John Gay, Bertolt Brecht, and Postcolonial Anti-nationalisms." *Modern Drama* 38 (Spring 1955).

Gay, John. *The Beggar's Opera.* Boston and New York: Houghton Mifflin, 1939.

McNeff, Stephen. "The Threepenny Opera." In *The Cambridge Companion to Brecht*, edited by Peter Thomson and Glendyr Sacks. Cambridge: Cambridge University Press, 1994.

Slonimsky, Nicolas, and Laura Kuhn. "Kurt Weill." In

PLAYS

1922 Baal

1922 Drums in the Night

1924 Edward the Second (Leben Eduards des Zweiten von England; with Feuchtwanger)

1927 In the Cities' Jungle (Im Dickicht der Städte)

1927 A Man Is a Man (Mann ist Mann)

1929 The Threepenny Opera

1929 The Rise and Fall of the City of Mahagonny

1932 St. Joan of the Stockyards

1941 Mother Courage and Her Children

1948 The Good Person of Setzuan

1948 The Caucasian Chalk Circle

1956 The Life of Galileo

1957 The Resistible Ascent of Arturo Ui (Der aufhaltsame Aufstieg des Arturo Ui)

POETRY

1927 Manual of Piety (Die Hauspostille)

1934 Songs, Poems, Choruses (Lieder, Gedichte, Chöre)

SCREENPLAYS

1943 Hangmen Also Die

FICTION

1937 The Threepenny Novel (Der Dreigroschenroman)

1949 Tales from the Calendar (Kalendergeschichten)

NONFICTION

1949 A Short Organum for the Theatre (Kleines Organon für das Theater)

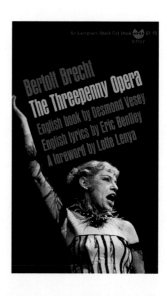

Baker's Biographical Dictionary of Musicians, edited by Nicolas Slonimsky and Laura Kuhn. New York: Schirmer Books, 2001.

MOTHER COURAGE AND HER CHILDREN

Genre: Ballad opera
Subgenre: Satirical tragicomedy
Published: New York, 1941
Time period: 1618–1648
    (the Thirty Years' War)
Setting: Various locations in Sweden, Poland, and Germany

Themes and Issues. *Mother Courage and Her Children* criticizes people who pit their religious beliefs against others' religious beliefs and people who profit from war. Mother Courage is one such person; she lives off others' hardships. At the conclusion of one scene, she curses war but then goes on with her business. Brecht hoped theatergoers would forget neither the play's antiwar message nor the point Mother Courage makes in the "Song of the Great Capitulation" about ceasing to resist injustice (as she too often does!). For the world to improve, people must never give in to evil, even if doing so makes life better for them.

The Plot. The Thirty Years' War lasted from 1618 to 1648 as a tangle of dynastic, religious, and national rivalries kept the continent in turmoil. For approximately 12 of those years, Mother Courage sells supplies from a wagon. She does not care which side she serves. Her sons, Eilif and Swiss Cheese, pull the wagon. Though she wants to keep the boys safe, brave Eilif is swayed by a recruiting officer's promises. The trusting Swiss Cheese also enlists in the army. Daughter Kattrin, so traumatized by war she cannot speak, remains with Mother Courage.

Having lost track of Eilif, one day the old woman overhears him praised for heroism. Given their leaders' carelessness and stupidity, Mother Courage knows soldiers must be unusually brave or wise to stay alive. Coming from behind the tent, she surprises Eilif. Instead of praising him as the commander

does, she boxes Eilif's ear for risking his life to steal oxen from Catholic peasants.

Sometime later an enemy attack separates Mother Courage, Kattrin, and others from the Protestants. Desperate to help her other son, Swiss Cheese, who has been captured, Mother Courage tries selling her wagon. With enough money she could bribe the soldiers to free him. As she argues over a selling price, an ominous drum roll signals his execution. Accused by the Catholics of hiding him before his capture, Mother Courage denies ever knowing Swiss Cheese. To protest their treatment of her, she goes to the Catholic soldiers' captain. Her rage is short lived. In the "Song of the Great Capitulation," she sings that no matter how defiant we are, eventually "we march in lockstep with the rest," as she has done concerning Swiss Cheese's death.

When a temporary peace ensues, Mother Courage fears her business will collapse. By now she has gotten over her younger son's death. During the peace Eilif breaks into a peasant cottage, is caught, and is executed. His mother never learns about his death. Soon after she exults that war has begun again.

The resumption of war means the end of Kattrin, however. When Catholic troops prepare to attack the sleeping inhabitants of a village, Kattrin beats a drum to awake the villagers. When she refuses to stop, soldiers shoot her. All this time Mother Courage is in town preparing to sell her wares at daybreak. Later in the morning, she returns to find Kattrin. Eventually realizing her daughter is not sleeping but dead, Mother Courage covers the body with a rag, harnesses herself to the wagon, and calls to the passing regiment, "Hey! Take me with you!"

Analysis. Mother Courage is one of the most intriguing characters in modern drama. A cold-hearted businesswoman bargaining for every cent, she is also at times compassionate and sympathetic, a mother trying only to keep her family together. Brecht began the play four weeks after the start of World War II on September 1, 1939. The war kept him from at-

Lotte Lenya in a 1965 production of *Mother Courage and Her Children* at the Ruhr Festival in West Germany. With her sons dead, Mother Courage is left to pull her wagon. Lenya, the wife of Kurt Weill, became famous singing "Alabama Song" in *Mahagonny*. She admired Brecht as a director and said he helped shape her performance: "Kurt gave me the singing style and Brecht gave me the movements." She went on to an international career, but German critics would pan her Mother Courage: they preferred Brecht's widow, Helene Weigel, who had made the role her own.

tending the play's Zurich premiere, where reviewers compared Mother Courage to Niobe in Greek myth. Niobe is turned to stone while weeping for her slain children. Wishing to make Mother Courage harder edged, less Niobe-like, for the play's Berlin opening, Brecht changed her character. The new Mother Courage was even more determined to profit from war. Brecht wrote that "to help performances," nearly everyone onstage must recognize that what attracts Mother Courage is "the purely commercial character of the war." The Brecht scholar Eric Bentley argues that the play is not a war play but a "business play."

SOURCES FOR FURTHER STUDY

Horwich, Cara Mary. *Survival in "Simplicissimus" and "Mother Courage."* New York: Peter Lang, 1996.

Stern, Guy. "Enriching *Mother Courage*." *Communications of the International Brecht Society*, June 1996.

Woodland, Ronald S. "The Danger of Empathy in *Mother Courage*." *Modern Drama* 15 (Sept. 1972).

THE GOOD PERSON OF SETZUAN

Genre: Ballad opera
Subgenre: Tragicomic parable
Published: Minneapolis, 1948
Time period: Premodern China
Setting: Semimythical, "half-Westernized city of Setzuan"

Themes and Issues. When people are sick or starving, it is difficult to remain good. For people to be virtuous, political and economic systems must change. A new method of existence would be free of both government corruption and the economic exploitation of one person by another. As Brecht asks at the conclusion of *The Good Person of Setzuan*, however, When even the gods can offer no help, where will this method be found?

The Plot. Three weary gods are sent to earth to seek enough good people to allow the world to remain as it is. While here they need a place to stay. Only Shen Te, a prostitute, takes them in. Pleased with her, the gods encourage her to continue to be good. She would like to be good, but she needs money if she is to help herself and others. Little can be done without money.

The gods give her a small sum with which she rents a tobacco shop. She feeds the poor and saves an unemployed pilot, Yang Sun, from committing suicide. Soon her relatives, her landlady, and others are taking advantage of her. Realizing how greedy and cruel people are, Shen Te disguises herself as a male cousin, who will be more hard-hearted in his dealings.

Unaware that Shen Te has disguised herself, the unemployed pilot, now her boyfriend, speaks ill of her to a newcomer, Mr. Shui Ta (Shen Te disguised). Still believing in the pilot's goodness despite what she has just heard him say about her, Shen Te sends him away to bribe an official to let him fly airplanes. Realizing she is pregnant with the pilot's child, Shen Te "vanishes." Meanwhile, people notice that Mr. Shui Ta is getting heavy.

Alerted to Shen Te's disappearance, the police suspect Shui Ta has imprisoned his cousin. In a trial before the three old gods, Shui Ta reveals who "he" is. Finding that Shui Ta is Shen Te, the gods ascend on a pink cloud, encouraging Shen Te to continue being good in a system where only money counts. Wondering how someone remains virtuous for long in such a world, Shen Te's last word to the gods is "Help!"

Analysis. Parables, whether told as stories or plays, illustrate moral or religious principles. The parable form suited epic theater. To emphasize that Shen Te can be good only by being bad part of the time as Shui Ta, Brecht set the play in a vague half-Western, half-Asian location and at no specific time. Thus, audiences would not have to trouble over questions of historical or geographical accuracy. They could pay closer attention to Shen Te's, to humanity's, plight: how any person can remain totally good yet stay alive with poverty and economic exploitation everywhere. No heavenly solution is to be expected. Like government officials, the gods are content to maintain the status quo. If dissatisfied people become too aware of their suffering, they can revolt against conditions. The gods offer tired phrases of comfort. Just as governments do, the gods tell Shen Te she is temporarily confused about matters, that they have faith in her, and that she is strong.

SOURCES FOR FURTHER STUDY

Fuegi, John. "The Alienated Woman: Brecht's *The Good Person of Setzuan.*" In *Essays on Brecht: Theater and Politics,* edited by Siegfried Mews and Herbert Kunst. Chapel Hill: University of North Carolina Press, 1974.

Kleber, Pia. *Exceptions and Rules: Brecht, Planchon, and "The Good Woman of Szechuan."* New York: Peter Lang, 1987.

Lug, Sieglinde. "The 'Good Woman' Demystified." *Communications of the International Brecht Society,* Nov. 1984.

Other Works

THE LIFE OF GALILEO (1956). Brecht worked on various versions of *The Life of Galileo* during a period of concern over the development of atomic weaponry. The play examines the scientist's responsibility to tell the truth. When Brecht began *Galileo* in 1938, a German physicist had succeeded in splitting the atom. When the English translation was written in 1945, the atom bomb had been dropped on Hiroshima, Japan. Brecht succeeded in giving a human face to science—that of a man who, despite greatness, was nevertheless weak and shallow.

Galileo was a seventeenth-century Italian physicist. His experiments reinforced the idea that the sun, not the earth, stood at the center of the universe. This view ran counter to the belief of the Catholic Church that man's central position on earth dictated that the sun revolved around him, the human reflection of God's handiwork. After remaining silent about his findings, Galileo, whose appetite for physical comfort matches his scientific zeal, speaks out. When church authorities threaten him with torture, Galileo, unwilling to risk physical pain, gives in to their demands. By not standing up for the truth, he ruins others' lives. Plagued by guilt for what he has done, he spends the rest of his life under house arrest. In the play's final scenes Galileo, old now, unenthusiastically copies out a record of his great earlier experiments.

Like Mother Courage, Brecht's Galileo is at times high-minded and strong, at other times vain, immoral, and weak. The play's force comes from the struggle between Galileo and the church and between Galileo and his appetites.

THE RISE AND FALL OF THE CITY OF MAHAGONNY (1929). In the Brecht-Weill opera *The Rise and Fall of the City of Mahagonny,* a newcomer, Paul Ackermann, offers a plan to help Mahagonny grow: Make it a city without rules. A screen lights with messages before each scene. One message lists Mahagonny's new temptations. Sampling the different pleasures in Mahagonny, one man eats himself to death. Another, a boxer, dies in a fight in a boxing ring. Brecht's point is that Mahagonny is any place where people make money indulging others' desires.

Eager to try different delights, Paul Ackermann gets drunk and makes light of a threatening hurricane. He buys everyone drinks with money he does not have. On the screen there is seen the projection of an arrow showing the storm as it bears down on Mahagonny. When just three minutes away, the storm veers in a half circle around the city. This action is comically projected on the screen.

Unable to pay the whiskey bill, Paul Ackermann is led to an electric chair onstage. When neither his lover nor his friends offer to pay his bill, Mrs. Begbick and the gang of criminals running Mahagonny sentence Paul Ackermann to die for singing a cheerful song during the hurricane threat, among other "crimes." As in most Brecht plays, to be penni-

A production of *Mahagonny* at the Sadler's Wells Theatre in London. Alaska Joe Wolf (played by Leon Greene) is down, Trinity Moses (played by Inia Te Wiata) is standing, and a projection of Nikita Khruschev makes a point. Using photos and film footage was one of Brecht's devices for, in theory, breaking up the illusion of reality so that audiences would think instead of feel.

less is the worst crime in a capitalist system. After Paul's death Mahagonny burns while its inhabitants sing about money. Spared the hurricane, the city is destroyed by the corruption of its citizens.

THE CAUCASIAN CHALK CIRCLE (1948).

Less than a year before the first professional production of *The Caucasian Chalk Circle* in 1948, Brecht appeared before the House Committee on Un-American Activities. That body was investigating communist influences in the Hollywood movie industry. Brecht, a communist for decades, had lived in California for six years. Not a few critics and editors considered his new play un-American because of

its view of property ownership. Should the will of an individual be greater than the will of the political state?

In a prologue set in 1945, Soviet comrades on a collective farm must decide who will work in a particularly fertile valley. With the Nazis gone, should the land be returned to those raised on it? Or should the land be given to those who will make better agricultural use of it? The second group wins out. The original tenants happily give up the valley. Good communists, their wishes are secondary to the wishes of the Soviet state.

Following the prologue, the play goes back in time a thousand years. During a fierce revolution a governor's wife abandons her baby,

Michael. Grusha, a peasant woman, saves Michael. In time, however, the governor's wife wants her son back: He is heir to the family wealth. A judge finally places the baby in a chalk circle, telling the two women that whoever first pulls him out of the circle keeps him. Though the rich wife wins her son back, the judge changes his mind and gives Michael to the honest, loving Grusha, who will raise Michael better. The land will be better for having its new tenants, and the baby will be better for having its new guardian. Individuals submit in order to further the good of the state.

Resources

Brecht's papers are at the Bertolt Brecht Archive in Berlin. They are administered by the German Academy of the Arts. Other institutions and organizations of interest to students of Bertolt Brecht include the following:

Facets Multi-Media, Inc. This Chicago-based company offers 16 Brecht-related videos for sale. Included are the 1931 film *The Threepenny Opera,* directed by G. W. Pabst and starring Lotte Lenya, Kurt Weill's wife. Brecht worked on the script with two other writers. When his film treatment was rejected, he distanced himself from the project. The 1963 film version of the play is also available from Facets, as is a video of the Salzburg (Austria) Festival production of *The Rise and Fall of the City of Mahagonny* (http://www.facets.org).

International Brecht Society. Based at the University of Wisconsin-Madison, the society promotes Brecht's work by attempting to maintain Brecht as "a living force in the theater" and as a force in contemporary culture and politics. The International Brecht Society publishes the *Brecht Yearbook,* which includes scholarly articles on Brecht research, most of them in English, as well as book reviews. The society also publishes *Communications of the International Brecht Society,* which features shorter articles on productions of Brecht's plays and on related events (http://polyglot.lss.wisc.edu/german/brecht/).

ANTHONY BUKOSKI

Index

Page numbers in **boldface** type indicate article titles. Page numbers in *italic* type indicate illustrations.